The Telephone Book

The AT&T Guide to Installing Telephones and Accessories

AT&T
5 Wood Hollow Road
Parsippany, NJ 07054

Notice: This book conforms to all FCC rules in effect as of the date of publication. It is your responsibility, however, to be aware of any local regulations that may affect modifications to the telephone wiring in your home.

Library of Congress Catalog Card Number: 85-73770

ISBN Number: 0-932764-11-8

Second printing, April, 1989

First published 1986 by AT&T, 5 Wood Hollow Road, Parsippany, NJ 07054 USA

Contents

1. What you should know before you start 1

2. Planning your home telephone system 10

3. Installing modular telephones and accessories 17

4. Converting older outlets to modular 29

5. Home telephone wiring 39

6. Installing modular jacks 61

7. Testing and troubleshooting 73

8. Telephones and accessories 78

9. Quick reference to AT&T wiring products 81

Glossary of terms 87

Index 93

Introduction

First, a word of encouragement. Nothing in this book is difficult to do. If you have a telephone — any telephone — in your home, it's now possible to modify or extend your telephone system quickly and easily. You can do it yourself, and it takes no special expertise or equipment.

The secret is simplicity. The wide selection of AT&T modular wiring products is designed for fast home installation by anyone. Everything plugs into everything else. No wire splicing or soldering is required to do anything in this book. Installing a new telephone can be as simple as taking it home and plugging it in. A screwdriver and a Saturday afternoon may be all you need to completely rewire your home.

Why it is possible to do your own telephone wiring is a longer story. It has to do with new regulations too complex to be described here. But the result is that now you can have full control over the telephones in your home. And despite 100 years of remarkable advances — from wooden boxes with cranks to the sleek electronic sophistication of today — this may be remembered as the most significant change in the American telephone system.

Today you have almost complete freedom to modify and improve your home telephone system. You can replace old-style telephones, add new phones and accessories, even rewire your entire home to accommodate advanced systems for computers, home security, or energy management. The result is more convenience, at far less cost to install and maintain, than ever before possible.

To help you along, this book is written in plain, non-technical terms to guide you through just about any telephone installation job. You don't need to know anything at all about telephones and wiring; and what you **do** need to know is explained simply, with clearly marked illustrations.

For the best results, we recommend using high-quality AT&T

wiring products. When properly installed they will provide safe, trouble-free service. Each product contains illustrated, step-by-step instructions to make any wiring job quick and easy. Instead of simply repeating the instructions given with each telephone product, this book is written to help you choose which components will best meet your needs for the job you want to do.

We'll help you evaluate your existing system to determine how it can be improved, recommend alternatives, and help you choose the best location for new phones. We'll describe the many modular accessories now available. If you're handy with tools, you may want to add the professional touches that can make your system more versatile and attractive. We'll help you there, too, with tips and advice from four generations of AT&T experts.

If you have a problem installing any of these products, just call us at 1 800 222-3111. The call is toll-free, and we'll be glad to help with installation advice and more information on any AT&T product.

For your convenience this book is organized into chapters based on specific tasks. If you already have modular outlets, for example, you can skip forward to Chapter 3 for information on installing new modular phones. If you want to replace older telephones with new modular phones, you'll find everything you need to know in Chapter 4.

Before doing anything, however, you should read the first chapter, "What You Should Know Before You Start." It briefly explains a few important points that determine what you can, and cannot, do. If you're not sure what you want to do, Chapter 2 will show you some of the many quick and easy changes and additions you can make to your home telephone system using AT&T wiring products.

A Glossary of terms begins on page 87. Here you will find short definitions of words or phrases that may be unfamiliar or puzzling to you. An Index, which begins on page 93, gives page references for specific items and procedures.

What you should know before you start

Installing your own telephones is easier than you may have thought. Using this book and a few AT&T wiring products, making modifications to any home telephone system is simple, safe, and inexpensive. But before you get started, there are a few things you should consider.

Important safety instructions

Always be careful when working with the telephone wiring in your home. By following these guidelines, you can greatly extend the versatility of your home telephone system with confidence and safety.

1 Never work with an active telephone line. The line contains a constant, low-level electrical current. This current is unlikely to cause any injury, but a slightly higher current is used to ring the telephone. This means that an incoming call can produce an unpleasant shock. Disconnect your wiring at the network interface while working, and wait until your wiring job is completed before connecting any new wiring to an active jack or interface.

If you do not have a network interface that can be disconnected, take all telephone handsets off the hook and set them aside while you work. Listen until you hear a dial tone, before you begin working. Ignore any other sounds such as a loud buzzing tone and recorded messages telling you to hang up.

2 Never handle bare wires or screws. Always hold the insulated portion of wires and use insulated tools.

3 Never work with telephone wiring during a thunderstorm, or when lightning is nearby.

4 Persons with pacemakers should never work with telephone wiring.

5 Telephones with lighted dials carry a low-voltage electrical current. Most draw power from the telephone line, but some are powered by a low-voltage transformer that should be disconnected before you work with any wiring. Check the electrical outlets near your phone; if you find a small, cube-shaped transformer, unplug it while you are working.

6 Telephones are not to be used near water. Never install telephone jacks in locations that would permit someone to use a telephone near a bath tub, laundry tub, wash bowl, kitchen sink, swimming pool, or in wet areas such as a damp basement.

7 If you must drill through or cut into walls to install any product, use caution to avoid hidden pipes, ducts and wiring. Never try to penetrate a wall near an electrical outlet.

8 Avoid placing loose telephone wires and cords in exposed areas where they could create a tripping hazard. Chapter 5 describes many ways to conceal and protect wires for a safer and more attractive installation.

Telephone regulations

Even though you now have much more freedom to do what you want with your telephones, there are still some restrictions. The changes you are allowed to make to the telephones and wiring in your home are determined by three organizations:

The Federal Communications Commission creates policies and regulations that affect the national telephone system, and all information in this book conforms to FCC guidelines as of the date of publication. Two other organizations, the **local telephone company** and **state public service commission** also have established rules that vary widely from state to state. You should be aware of these local rules before modifying or adding to any telephone wiring in your home.

You may be required to notify your local telephone company when you install any telephone equipment. The information you must give the telephone company is usually printed on a manufacturer's label on the underside of the telephone. Look for two numbers: the **FCC registration number** and the **ringer equivalence number** (or REN; see page 91).

Your point of demarcation

Two FCC regulations must be complied with before you install any new wiring. However, since local policies vary with regard to these regulations, you should call your local telephone company to determine the policy in your area.

One requirement is that a **point of demarcation** be established before you install any new wiring. This is a place in your home wiring beyond which you agree to install and maintain your own wiring and connections. The telephone company will continue to own and maintain all wiring from the central office up to that point in your home. (See Figure 1-1.)

The FCC also requires that you have some means of disconnecting your home wiring from the telephone company network. In some cases an existing outlet is used for this purpose. In other homes a **network interface** (a type of modular jack specifically designed for this purpose) is used instead.

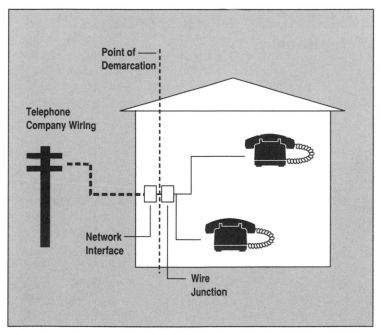

Figure 1-1 Establishing a point of demarcation

In many homes, a network interface has already been installed by the telephone company. To determine whether you have one, look near the main electrical panel, or near the point where telephone wiring first enters your home (often in the attic or basement; in apartments, often in the kitchen or in a closet near an exterior door).

If you don't already have a network interface, the telephone company can install one for you. There is usually a one-time installation charge, but the cost is modest compared to the advantages it provides. The network interface provides a safe and convenient way to disconnect all the telephones in your home while making repairs or modifications to your system. (See Figure 1-2.)

How many telephones?

A **ringer equivalence number** assigned to all telephones helps determine how many phones you can install in your home. The telephone company usually provides you with enough power to ring

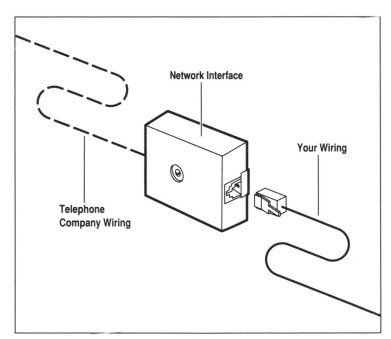

Figure 1-2 The network interface

five telephones per line. However, some telephones require more ringing power than others. The amount of power each phone needs is expressed as a ringer equivalence number (REN) that can usually be found on a label on the underside of the telephone. Most phones have a REN of one (1.0) or less.

To find out how many telephones you can install, simply add up the REN numbers of all your phones; if the total is less than five, you should have no problems.

If the total is more than five, there might not be enough power to ring all your telephones. The phones will still work — that is, you can still make and receive calls — but some of them might not ring when you get an incoming call. If this is inconvenient, you can either disconnect phones you don't often use, or replace some of them with phones that have a lower REN and require less ringing power.

Pulse and tone:
The two types of telephone service

The service provided by your telephone company can be one of two basic kinds: **pulse dialing** (rotary) or **tone dialing** (touch-tone).

Make sure you know which type of service you have before buying a new telephone or planning any changes. If you're not sure, your local telephone company can tell you whether you have pulse or tone-dialing service.

Pulse dialing is usually associated with rotary telephones (phones with a round dial). If you have pulse-dialing service, only pulse-dialing telephones will work in your home. Check carefully before you buy. Some telephones are designed only for tone dialing, and will not work with pulse-dialing service. Others are designed to work with either type of service.

In most areas you can request that the local telephone company change your service from pulse to tone dialing. Although tone-dialing service costs a few dollars more per month, it will allow you a much greater variety of options.

Tone dialing (also called touch-tone) is a newer method of dialing using a keypad with twelve buttons instead of a rotary dial. Tone-dialing phones are easier to use and dial much more quickly than pulse telephones. They are also much more versatile. Tone-dialing telephones allow you access to computer services, telephone banking services, long-distance services, voice-mail networks and the automated answering systems used by many larger organizations to route calls quickly.

Any telephone can be used with tone-dialing service, but if you have tone-dialing service, make sure you buy true tone-dialing phones. Don't judge by the appearance of the phone; many telephones that have push buttons are actually pulse-dialing phones. Although they will work with tone-dialing service, they dial just as slowly as a rotary telephone and won't allow you to take full advantage of the tone-dialing service you're buying from the telephone company.

Types of telephone connections

The way phones are connected to the telephone wiring in your home will often determine how you'll proceed with any wiring modifications or additions.

Most telephones installed after 1974 are connected with **modular jacks and plugs.** These connections are easily recognized; if your phones are connected to the wall jacks shown here with miniature clip-in plugs, they are the newer modular type. Chapter 3 explains how to install new modular telephones if you already have modular jacks. To install extra jacks, see Chapters 5 and 6. (See Figure 1-3.)

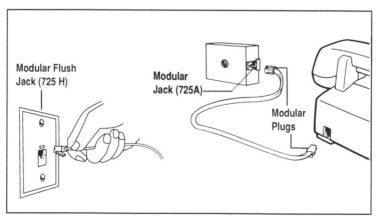

Figure 1-3 Modular jacks and plugs

Many telephones installed before 1974 cannot be unplugged. These telephones are connected directly to an outlet mounted either inside the wall or on a baseboard. Except for their external appearance these types of connections are identical, and both are referred to as **hard-wired connections**. If you have any hard-wired telephones, Chapter 4 describes several ways to convert the existing connection into a jack that can be used with newer, modular telephones. AT&T offers a variety of modular converters that can be installed in minutes without extensive rewiring. (See Figure 1-4.)

It is sometimes difficult to determine which kind of connector is used for **wall telephones**. If your wall phone is one of the types shown here, it is probably hard wired. In Chapter 4, you'll find information on how to remove a hard-wired wall telephone and replace it with a modern, modular wall phone. (See Figure 1-5.)

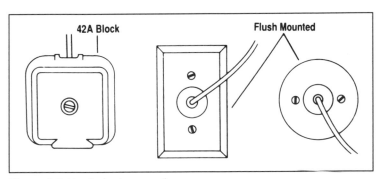

Figure 1-4 Hard-wired connections

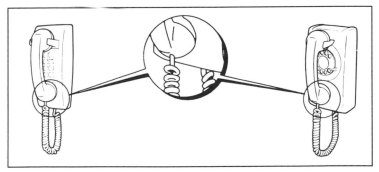

Figure 1-5 Hard-wired wall telephones

Four-prong jacks, as shown here, are common in many homes for connecting extension telephones. (See Figure 1-6.) These must be converted for use with newer modular telephones and other devices. AT&T offers a **Plug-In Converter** for this purpose. (See Figure 1-7.) For a more attractive appearance, you can instead replace a four-prong jack with a new modular jack. Both procedures are described in Chapter 4.

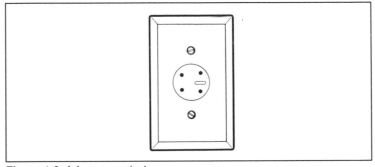

Figure 1-6 A four-prong jack

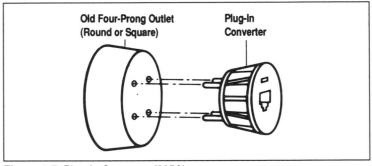

Figure 1-7 Plug-In Converter (225A)

Tools you'll need

Many of the projects described in this book can be completed in minutes without tools by using AT&T plug-in wiring products. Others require a few standard home-maintenance tools, which are listed with each project described in the book.

A most useful tool is the **Telephone Line Tester with Slitter** (953B), available wherever AT&T wiring products are sold. This is an inexpensive tool that can simplify many wiring jobs, and greatly reduce the possibility of accidental damage to telephone wiring and components. (See Figure 1-8.)

This versatile tool can be used to strip insulation from telephone wire, to break out wire-channel tabs in modular components such as jacks and wire junctions, and to install telephone conductors in many telephone products. It also functions as a multi-purpose line tester that allows you to check any jack installation or wiring job before installing telephones. The tester can be used to check for line problems, and can help avoid the expense of a service call if you don't have a second telephone to verify whether the trouble is in your telephone or in the line.

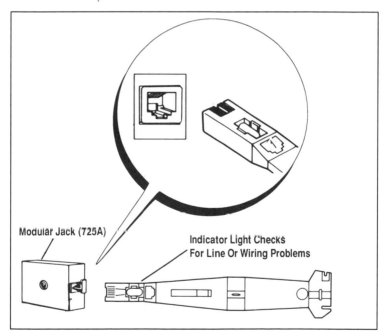

Modular Jack (725A)

Indicator Light Checks
For Line Or Wiring Problems

Figure 1-8 Telephone Line Tester

2 Planning your home telephone system

Depending on the wiring you now have, adding a new telephone may be as simple as plugging in an extension cord for a table lamp. In homes already equipped with at least one modular jack, telephone extension cords can be attached in minutes (see Chapter 3). Older homes often require conversion from hard-wired phones to a modular wiring system. This, too, can be done quickly using the modular adapters described in Chapter 4.

For a more attractive appearance in either case, or to add a more versatile system of telephones and accessories, Chapters 5 and 6 explain how to extend your system by installing a variety of modular jacks, junctions and concealed wiring.

But before you begin, take a few minutes to look over the illustrations in this chapter. The sample telephone wiring plans shown here will help you decide what to do and where to start. And along the way you'll learn valuable tips on how to plan your wiring to meet both present and future needs.

Limiting factors

Most of the ideas presented in this book require few or no visible alterations to your home, and those that do are described in Chapters 5 and 6. However, if you rent or lease your home, always check with the owner before modifying or adding telephone wiring and accessories. Some lease contracts prohibit certain modifications.

Also, as you read over the following suggestions, plan jack positions to minimize wire length. In most homes, the use of AT&T wire and accessories will assure reliable service for almost any application. But remember that resistance to electrical current increases with wire length. A good rule of thumb is that no jacks should be farther than 200 feet from the point where wiring first enters your home.

Basic wiring plans

Since you are responsible for maintaining any wiring you install beyond the point of demarcation, it pays to plan your wiring carefully. There are two basic kinds of wiring plans, and each has distinct advantages, depending on your needs.

A more complete description of these wiring plans is given in Chapter 5. As you read over this chapter, keep in mind that the wiring plan you choose may limit, or greatly extend, the conveniences you might want to install later.

Loop wiring is suitable for small homes where only a few jacks will be installed. In a loop system the wiring starts at a network interface, runs from jack to jack, and loops back to the interface. A loop system is the easiest and least expensive type of wiring system to install.

Home-run wiring, although it requires slightly more time and materials to install, is often preferred in larger homes because of its reliability and versatility. This system involves routing each jack separately to a common connecting point in the home.

Exposed or concealed wiring

Each of the suggestions in the following sample wiring plan can be installed in a variety of ways. (See Figure 2-1.) To install an extension telephone quickly and easily, a line-cord extension can simply be routed along a baseboard. For a more permanent connection, telephone station wire can be routed the same way or can be concealed beneath baseboards, under carpet edges, within walls, or beneath floors.

In the following chapters you'll find complete descriptions of each kind of wiring, and advice on many installation techniques ranging from the simplest to the most professional.

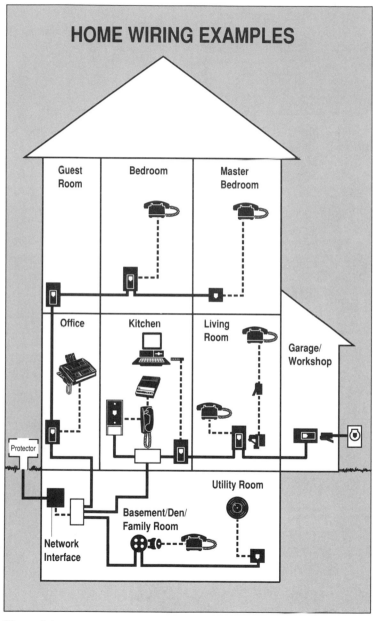

Figure 2-1

12

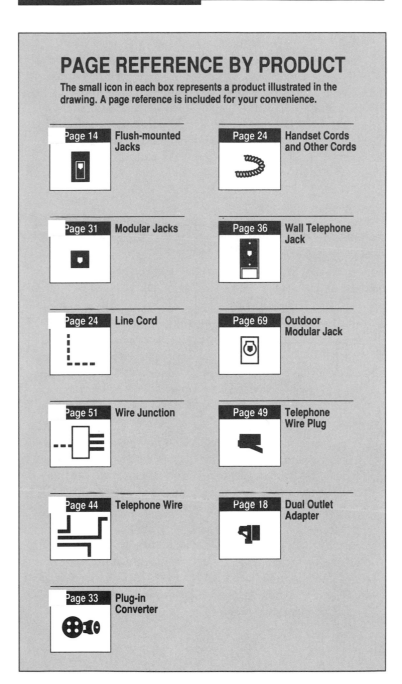

PAGE REFERENCE BY PRODUCT

The small icon in each box represents a product illustrated in the drawing. A page reference is included for your convenience.

Page 14	Flush-mounted Jacks	Page 24	Handset Cords and Other Cords
Page 31	Modular Jacks	Page 36	Wall Telephone Jack
Page 24	Line Cord	Page 69	Outdoor Modular Jack
Page 51	Wire Junction	Page 49	Telephone Wire Plug
Page 44	Telephone Wire	Page 18	Dual Outlet Adapter
Page 33	Plug-in Converter		

Home wiring ideas

Page 12 illustrates some of the many installations possible using
AT&T wiring accessories. Of course, since ringer equivalence
limits the number of telephones you can install, most homes will
not have all the telephone equipment shown here. But in many
cases, extra jacks might be desirable for convenience in locations
where a telephone is often needed temporarily, such as a guest
bedroom, a workshop or utility room, the garage, or an outdoor
patio. Any number of jacks can be installed as long as the ringer
equivalence of telephones and accessories connected at any one
time does not exceed five.

Each feature shown on page 12 is only briefly described here.
For more detailed information, refer to the chapter indicated for the
accessories you want to install. Each AT&T product mentioned is
followed by an identifying number to help you choose the correct
product for each application.

1 Connected to the network interface, where wiring enters the
home, is a **Wire Junction** (742B). In most homes wired for
modular jacks, this junction will be the starting point of all
telephone wiring. From this junction you can route up to three
wire paths to connect jacks or additional wire junctions. To
convert an older wiring system to modular, see Chapter 4.
Additional wire junctions can be added at any point to simplify
your wiring.

2 From the first wire junction, **Telephone Station Wire** extends
to each jack in the home. This durable wire contains four color-
coded conductors to make jack installation simple and quick
(see Chapter 5).

3 A **Line Cord** is an alternative to station wire for limited uses.
Unlike station wire, the extension line cord simply plugs into an
existing modular jack. This allows you to use a telephone in a
different location (up to 25 feet away) without installing a new
jack. With a **Dual Outlet Adapter** (267A2), an extension cord
can be used to add a second telephone in a room with only one
modular jack (see Chapter 3).

4 Flush-mounted **Modular Jack**s install in the wall for a neat,
unobtrusive appearance. Several types are available. In homes
with older wiring systems, hard-wired phone connections can
be converted to modular with a **Modular Jack Converter**
(725F; see Chapter 4). In new homes that are prewired for
modular telephones, **Prewire Flush Jacks** (725H) can be
quickly installed in existing junction boxes. If your home does
not have these junction boxes already installed in the walls, you
can install a flush-mounted **Modular Jack** (725E) using
existing wiring or new station wire (see Chapter 6). All three
jacks have quick-connect wire terminals for easy installation.

5 For quick installation without running wire inside walls, a
surface mounted **Modular Jack** (725A) can be installed on a
wall or baseboard (see Chapter 6). In older homes, hard-wired
phone connections can be converted to modular with a
Modular Jack Converter (725C; see Chapter 4).

6 **Plug-in Converters** (225A) convert older four-prong jacks for
use with modular telephones (see Chapter 4). The converter can
be left in the older jack, or can be removed; this is useful, for
example, to allow a new modular phone to be moved from
room to room without rewiring many four-prong jacks.

7 **Dual Outlet Adapters** (267A2) allow two line cords to be
plugged into any modular jack. These adapters can be used to
add a second telephone or accessory in a room with only one
jack (see Chapter 3).   *(Continued)*

8 A **Modular Jack for Wall Telephones** (630B) can be used to install a new wall phone or to replace an existing hard-wired wall phone. In some new prewired homes, a prewired version of the **Modular Jack for Wall Telephones** (830A) can be connected to an existing junction box (see Chapter 6). If a modular jack is nearby, a **Phonemount** (730A) will allow you to install a new wall phone without running wires inside the wall (see Chapter 3).

Two convenient accessories are available for wall phones. A **Backboard** (191C), available in several colors to match most decors, can be snapped in place to eliminate any excess space between the phone and the wall. The versatile **Dual Outlet Adapter for Wall Telephones** (733A) allows you to connect a second telephone or accessory to any modular wall phone (see Chapters 3 and 6).

9 For outdoor use, an **Outdoor Modular Jack** (Z625WP4) provides a durable and weatherproof telephone connection.

10 To permit easy connection and disconnection of extension telephone jacks, a **Telephone Wire Plug** (700A4) connected to telephone wire can be plugged directly into any modular outlet. (NOTE: Telephone wire is intended for permanent installation; it should not be used as a substitute for line cord. See Chapter 5, page 44.)

11 Chapter 3 describes many kinds of line cords, handset cords and other plug-in accessories for modular telephones.

12 Chapter 8 describes many kinds of telephone equipment available from AT&T that can add security and convenience to your home. All can be quickly connected to any modular jack described in this book.

3 Installing modular telephones and accessories

For homes with modular jacks already installed, this chapter describes how to install new telephones and many plug-in accessory products now available from AT&T. To extend your system by adding additional wiring and jacks, see Chapters 5 and 6.

Before installing a new phone, make sure it has a label showing the FCC registration number and ringer equivalence number. You may be required to notify the local telephone company and report these numbers when you install a new telephone or accessory (see Chapter 1). After installing any new modular component, conduct the tests described in Chapter 7 to make sure it has been connected correctly.

Safety instructions

Please read the important safety instructions beginning on page 1 before working with any telephone products other than those that simply plug into an existing modular jack.

To install a modular desk phone

Connecting a modular desk telephone is as simple as plugging the new phone into a modular jack. (See Figure 3-1.) Insert the

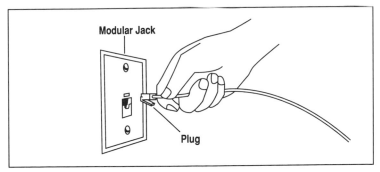

Figure 3-1 Installing a modular telephone

17

modular plug into the jack until it snaps firmly into place. To remove it, squeeze the clip and pull. Always pull only the clear plastic plug, never the line cord. After installation, lift the handset and listen to make sure you have a dial tone.

To add additional modular jacks

The easiest way to add an extension phone is to connect it to an existing jack. For a quick installation, this can be done in minutes using a **25-foot Extension Cord** and a **Dual Outlet Adapter** (267A2) as shown in Figure 3-2.

For a more permanent installation, use a surface-mounted or flush-mounted jack as shown on pages 63 and 64. (See Figure 3-3.) The **Modular Jack** (725A) can be attached directly to a wall or baseboard with two screws. The flush-mounted **Modular Jack**

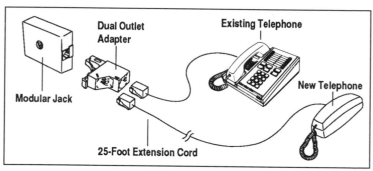

Figure 3-2 Connecting two telephones to the same jack

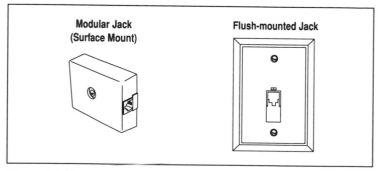

Figure 3-3 Types of modular jacks

(725E) is designed for mounting in a hollow wall for a more attractive appearance. Chapter 6 describes how each of these jacks can be connected with telephone station wire to any existing modular jack or wire junction. Self-adhesive **Telephone Wire Clips** can be used to protect and support wire routed along walls and other surfaces as shown on page 55. (See Figure 3-4.)

For a quick and easy way to add an additional telephone, the **Add-a-Jack** kit described in Chapter 6 includes all the wiring and hardware you need to install a new telephone jack. The kit is available in two versions for use with desk telephones or wall telephones.

To replace a wall telephone

Before replacing an existing wall phone, you must first determine which type of wall phone you already have. Compare your wall phone with those shown on page 20; if it is a hard-wired phone, turn to Chapter 4 for instructions on replacing it.

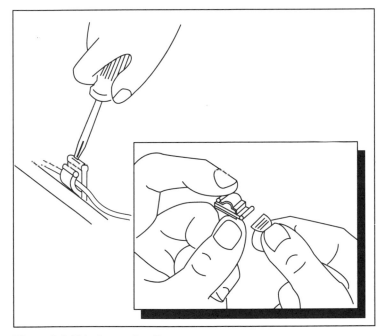

Figure 3-4 Telephone wire clips

Modular wall phones can be removed easily. One model plugs directly into the wall jack; another type has a short line cord between the telephone and the wall. Grasp the phone as shown below and lift up to remove it from the mounting studs. Pull it

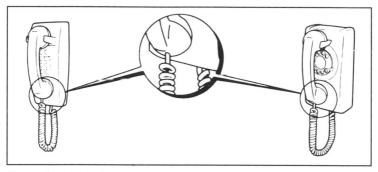

Figure 3-5 Hard-wired wall telephones

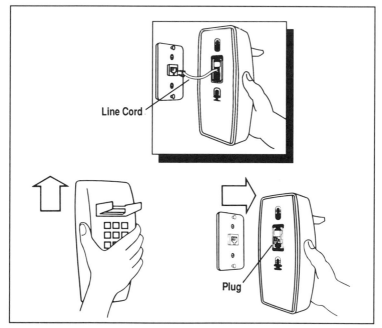

Line Cord

Plug

Figure 3-6 Removing modular wall phones

slightly away from the wall and check to see if it has a line cord that must be unplugged.

After removing a modular wall phone, installing a new one is quite simple, as shown below. Many newer phones require that you plug in a short line cord before mounting the phone. Others have a sliding modular plug permanently attached to the phone instead of a line cord. To install this type of phone, slide the plug down to the bottom of the slot and push the phone against the wall mounting plate so that the modular plug engages the jack. Lift the phone slightly up and onto the mounting studs, then push down until it locks in place. Be sure to follow the installation guidelines packaged with the telephone, since some have special mounting requirements.

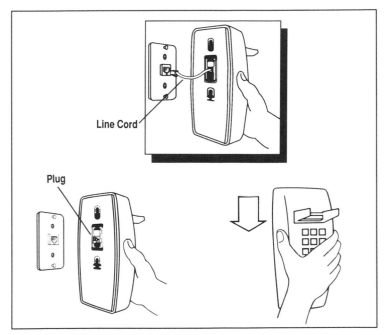

Line Cord

Plug

Figure 3-7 Installing modular wall phones

To install a jack for a new wall telephone

There are two ways to install a wall telephone where there is no jack. Chapter 6 describes how to install a permanent jack and connect it to your home's station wire. A wall-telephone version of the convenient **Add-a-Jack** kit can make this job easier by providing everything you need to install a new jack up to 50 feet from an existing jack.

There is a much faster alternative, however, if you want to install a wall telephone within six feet of an existing jack. The **Phonemount** (730A) attaches directly to the surface of any wall with two wood screws or anchor screws. Installation can usually be completed in minutes, using only a screwdriver. A six-foot modular line cord connected to the Phonemount plugs into any nearby modular jack to complete the connection.

To install the Phonemount more than six feet away from an existing jack, a **25-foot Extension Cord** can be used. Since loose cords can create a tripping hazard, use wire clips as shown on page 55 to route the cord along a wall or baseboard for a more attractive and safer installation.

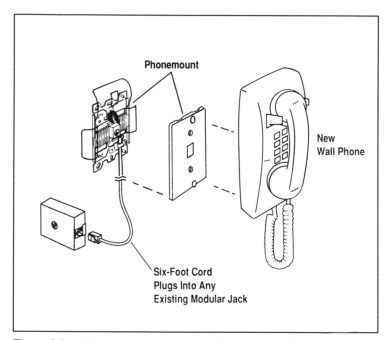

Figure 3-8 Using a Phonemount to install a modular wall phone

Modular wall telephone accessories

To add an extra telephone or accessory (such as an answering machine) near a wall phone, a **Dual Outlet Adapter** (733A) can be attached between the wall and the telephone as shown below. Most kinds of telephones and accessories can be connected directly to the additional jack on the bottom of the adapter.

For a more attractive appearance, a **Backboard** (191C) can be installed as shown below, to eliminate any noticeable space between the telephone and the wall. The backboard is also useful to conceal any wall or wallpaper discoloration revealed when an older wall phone is replaced with a smaller one. Backboards for wall telephones are available in several colors to match many decorating schemes.

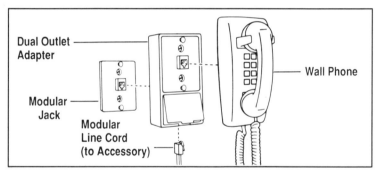

Dual Outlet Adapter

Modular Jack

Modular Line Cord (to Accessory)

Wall Phone

Figure 3-9 Using Dual Outlet Adapter to add an extra telephone

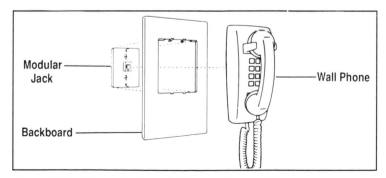

Modular Jack

Backboard

Wall Phone

Figure 3-10 Using a Backboard with a modular wall phone

Modular line cords

Most telephones, answering systems, facsimile machines and similar devices include a standard line cord for connection to a modular jack. You can replace any standard line cord with one of the special-purpose cords available from AT&T.

25-foot Decorator Line Cords, available in a wide variety of colors, are extra long to permit easy movement of a telephone throughout the room.

Clear Line Cords, designed to blend with any decor, are available in four lengths from two feet to 25 feet.

All replacement line cords have a modular plug on each end for a quick, secure connection. They are designed for compatibility with any device that uses standard line cords. There are some telephones that require special cords, however, and you should check carefully before you buy.

Modular handset cords

Handset cords can be used only to connect a handset to a telephone. Because handset cords are wired differently, and because their modular plugs are smaller than line-cord plugs, handset cords cannot be used to connect the telephone to a wall jack. Two types of cords are available to replace the standard handset cord on modular phones.

12-foot Handset Cords, available in many colors, save space by remaining neatly coiled when not in use.

25-foot Heavy Duty Handset Cords, also available in several colors, are resilient, coiled handset cords that can be extended for greater mobility. Because of their durable construction these cords are much more resistant to sagging, and retain their coiled shape even after repeated stretching to maximum length.

Modular adapters

For additional convenience, several kinds of plug-in adapters (shown on page 25) can be used to make your modular phone system more versatile.

A **Modular Coupler** (460A) joins two modular line cords to form one long line cord.

A **Dual Outlet Adapter** (267A2) allows two phones or acces-

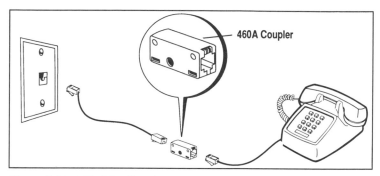

Figure 3-11 A Modular Coupler

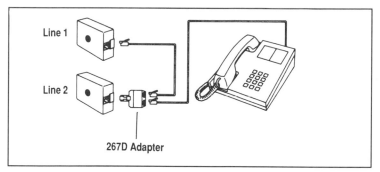

Figure 3-12 Using a Dual Line Adapter

sories to be plugged into any modular jack. This adapter is useful to add a second telephone in a room with only one jack; or to connect an answering system, facsimile machine, automatic dialer, or computer modem to a jack already used for a telephone.

If you have two telephone lines in separate jacks, a **Dual Line Adapter** (267D) can be used to bridge the two jacks so you can connect a two-line telephone.

Volume and noise control accessories

Several accessories are convenient for use in noisy environments, or for persons who have a hearing impairment.

The **Volume Control Handset** (G-6) can replace the handset of some modular phones. A built-in volume control allows you to adjust the handset to a comfortable listening level. (See Figure 3-13.)

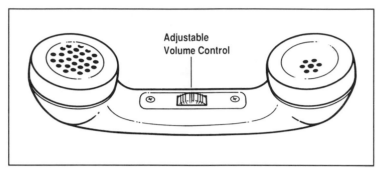

Figure 3-13 The Volume Control Handset

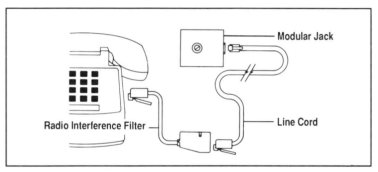

Figure 3-14 Using a Radio Interference Filter

The **In-line Amplifier** plugs in between the handset and the telephone to allow volume control of your existing handset. Self-adhesive strips are provided to attach the amplifier to a desk or to the telephone. The amplifier can be used with most modular telephones except those that have a dial or keypad in the handset. Power is provided by any standard electrical outlet.

The battery-powered **Portable Amplifier** is particularly con-venient to carry along for use in noisy locations such as airports and industrial facilities. This compact amplifier slips over the handset receiver of most telephones. A top-mounted control knob makes it easy to adjust the volume during conversations.

The **Radio Interference Filter** (Z100A) is designed to suppress unwanted noise from local AM radio stations that might be heard through your home telephone. This filter can also help to reduce annoyance from private citizen's band and ham radio transmitters.

An **Auxiliary Bell Ringer** (E1EM) provides a traditional bell ringing sound for use with newer telephones that have electronic ringers. The ringer can be mounted up to seven feet from the telephone using the standard line cord provided. With an optional extension cord, the ringer can be mounted up to 25 feet from the telephone, either indoors or in an outdoor location if protected from rain and snow. Volume is adjustable by setting a built-in control knob.

Hands-free accessories

Modular Headsets are ideal for those who use the telephone frequently while performing other tasks. Headsets are available in three models for use with standard, electronic, or multi-line telephones. Each includes a belt-mounted control console with volume control knob and an adjustable, lightweight headband designed to reduce fatigue.

For less-frequent use, **Shoulder Rests** provide a soft, non-slip surface to rest the handset on either shoulder comfortably. Shoulder rests are available in two designs to fit most modern handsets; each is available in a wide variety of colors.

AT&T cordless telephone accessories

Rechargeable **Replacement Batteries** can be used in any AT&T cordless telephone. These high-quality batteries are recommended to maintain the superior performance of AT&T cordless telephones. For worn or damaged cordless phones, **Replacement Antennas** can be installed to improve performance and restore the original attractive appearance. If the original antenna is removable, the replacement antenna can be installed quickly without tools. The **Cordless Carrying Case** is designed to fit all AT&T cordless telephones for convenience and protection. The case can be attached to a belt or to clothing for easy portability. An adjustable flap makes the case compatible with cordless telephones of many shapes and sizes.

Answering system tape cassettes

Three high-performance recording tapes are available for use with most telephone answering systems. Each is designed to exacting AT&T standards for extended life and clear voice quality.

The 30-second **Outgoing Message Tape** is an endless-loop tape for use with answering systems that accept standard-size tape cassettes. The 60-minute **Incoming Message Tape** is a leaderless tape providing 30 minutes' recording time per side for incoming messages. The 60-minute **Microcassette**, to record incoming messages, is designed for answering systems requiring smaller microcassette tapes.

Multi-purpose line tester & installation tool

The **Telephone Line Tester** with slitter (953B) is several tools in one. It can be plugged into any modular jack to check whether the jack or telephone wiring is working correctly. The tester also performs many other functions to aid in the installation of telephone wiring components (see pages 9 and 47).

Extending your modular system

The ideas presented in this chapter are limited to installations that can be completed quickly, using surface-mounted wiring and accessories. To add a more attractive system of flush-mounted jacks and concealed wiring, see Chapters 5 and 6. These two chapters offer many ideas for more extensive modular systems and helpful tips on how to install wiring within walls and cabinets, beneath floors, and in attics and crawl spaces.

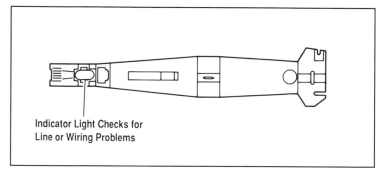

Indicator Light Checks for
Line or Wiring Problems

Figure 3-15 The Telephone Line Tester

4 Converting older outlets to modular

Since all new telephones and accessories are designed for use with modular jacks, you may have to convert to modular connections before adding new phones and jacks. This chapter describes several ways to modernize most older phone connections.

First, determine how your existing telephones are connected. Compare your telephone connections to those shown on page 20. There are three types of non-modular telephone connections.

1 The most common type of telephone installed before 1974 is referred to as **hard wired**, since the telephone cannot be unplugged. There are two kinds of hard-wired connections. The **42A block** is a small box attached directly to a all or baseboard. A line cord runs from the telephone into the 42A block. A **flush-mounted** connection has a round or rectangular faceplate covering a junction box concealed inside the wall. A line cord runs from the telephone through a hole in the center of the faceplate. (See Figure 4-1.)

2 There are several types of **hard-wired wall telephones**, but each can be identified easily by checking the handset cord. If the handset cord cannot be unplugged, the telephone is hard wired. (See Figure 4-2.)

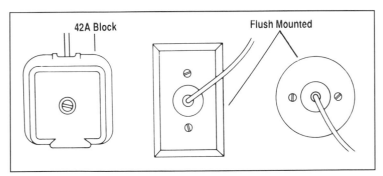

Figure 4-1 Non-modular telephone connections

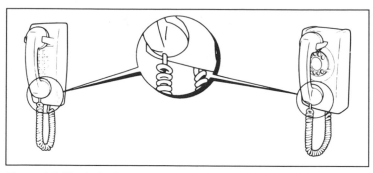

Figure 4-2 Hard-wired wall telephones

3 A type of outlet previously used for portable extension telephones is the **four-prong jack**. This type of jack may be mounted on a wall or baseboard, or flush mounted in a junction box covered by a plastic faceplate.

Any outlet can be quickly converted for use with modular telephones. Older telephones can also be converted for use with modular jacks. AT&T offers a variety of converters designed for each kind of older connection. Step-by-step installation instructions are included with each converter, but the following guidelines will help you determine which is best suited for your home.

After converting any existing connection, check to make sure the job has been done properly by conducting the tests described in Chapter 7.

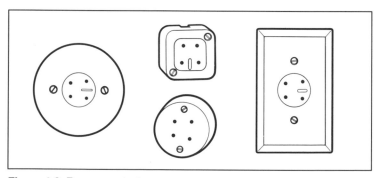

Figure 4-3 Four-prong jacks

Safety instructions

Please read the important safety instructions beginning on page 1 before converting older outlets or working with any telephone products other than those that simply plug into an existing modular jack.

Converting a 42A block to a modular jack

Tools: Screwdriver, Wire cutters or Scissors

Materials: Modular Jack Converter (725C)

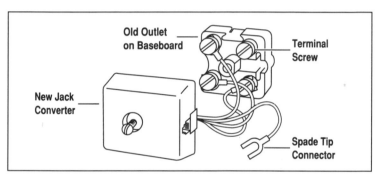

Figure 4-4 Modular Jack Converter (725C)

To convert a hard-wired connecting block, use a screwdriver to remove the cover, exposing four screw terminals. To disconnect your old telephone, the four wires leading from the block to the old telephone cord must be cut near the screw terminals; cut each wire individually, and be careful not to cut any other wires since they provide telephone service to the jack. Loosen the four terminal screws and attach each spade-tip connector to the appropriate terminal, using the color-coding of the wire insulation as a guide. Then attach the new cover provided with the converter.

If your 42A block is in an inconvenient location for a modular jack, there are a number of alternatives. You can convert the connecting block as described above, then route additional wire from it to a second modular jack in the desired location. Or you can completely remove the block and replace it with a modular jack. Both procedures are described in Chapters 5 and 6.

Converting a hard-wired junction box to a modular jack

Tools: Screwdriver, Wire cutters or Scissors

Materials: Modular Jack Converter, Flush Mounted (725F)

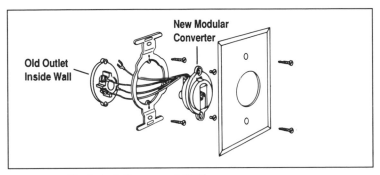

Figure 4-5 Flush Jack Converter (725F)

Some hard-wired telephones are connected to a junction box inside the wall, with the telephone line cord emerging from a round or rectangular faceplate. This converter replaces the hard-wired connection with a modular jack.

Use a screwdriver to remove the faceplate covering the junction box. Inside is a connecting block with four screw terminals. To remove your old telephone, the four wires leading from the outlet to the old telephone cord must be cut near the screw terminals; cut each of these wires individually, and be careful not to cut any other wires since they provide telephone service to the jack. Loosen the four terminal screws and attach each spade-tip connector to the appropriate terminal, using the color coding of the wire insulation as a guide.

Mount the new modular jack converter in the junction box with the two screws provided. To complete the installation, you can either mount the original faceplate or replace with a new one for a more attractive appearance.

Converting a four-prong outlet for modular use

Tools: None

Materials: Plug-In Converter, Portable, Four-prong to Modular (225A)

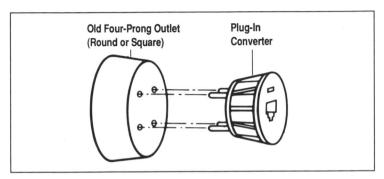

Old Four-Prong Outlet
(Round or Square)

Plug-In
Converter

Figure 4-6 Plug-In Converter (225A)

This converter plugs into any existing four-prong outlet to adapt it for use with any modular telephone. Because it does not permanently change the outlet, the converter can be unplugged at any time to reconnect your existing four-prong extension phone. If you have more than one four-prong outlet, you may want to buy more than one converter so that each outlet can be used for either four-prong or modular telephones.

Replacing a four-prong outlet with a modular jack

Tools: Screwdriver, Wire cutters or Scissors

Materials: Modular Jack (725A)or Modular Jack, Flush Mounted (725E)

For a more attractive appearance, or for more protection in locations where a protruding adapter could be damaged by furniture, you might want to remove a four-prong outlet and replace it with a modular jack. This will require more installation time than simply plugging in the adapter described above. However, there is another advantage to replacing the old outlet with a new modular jack. Built into each jack described here are special screw terminals that can be used as the starting point for an entire network of new modular

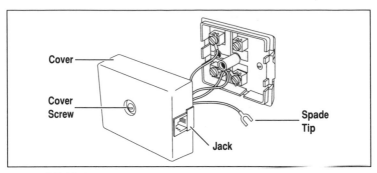

Figure 4-7 Modular Jack (725A)

jacks. Chapters 5 and 6 describe how to extend your modular system by connecting station wire to any existing modular jack.

The choice of jack will depend on how your four-prong outlet is mounted. If the outlet is mounted on the surface of a wall, baseboard or cabinet, it can be most easily replaced by a surface-mounted modular jack (725A). First, remove the four-prong outlet, then use wire cutters to cut off the four wires attached to the outlet so that no uninsulated wire is exposed. Two screws are provided to install the new modular jack in place of the old four-prong outlet. No wire stripping is necessary to attach the four conducting wires to the modular jack. Just insert each wire into a slot beneath the appropriate color-coded screw terminal; when the screws are tightened the wire insulation is pierced to create secure connections.

Flush-mounted four-prong outlets are most easily replaced with a modular jack designed for flush mounting (725E). First, remove the existing faceplate to expose the four-prong outlet in the junction box. Then cut the four wires attached to the outlet so that no uninsulated wire is exposed. The wires are attached to the new modular jack as described above; no wire stripping is necessary. The modular jack has a new faceplate built in.

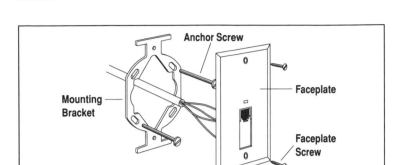

Figure 4-8 Flush Jack (725E)

Converting older telephones for use with modular jacks

Tools: Screwdriver

Materials: Line Cord Converter (732B)

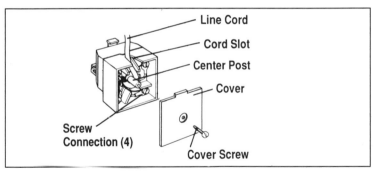

Figure 4-9 Line Cord Converter (732B)

The Line Cord Converter is a modular plug that quickly converts any older table telephone, either the hard-wired or four-prong plug type, for use with modular jacks.

The conversion is easier if you don't cut the wires when you first disconnect the phone from the wall. Instead, loosen the terminal screws in the hard-wired outlet or the old four-prong plug and remove the exposed wires. This prevents your having to strip the wires to connect the modular plug, since the correct amount of insulation has already been stripped from each wire. (If the telephone line cord has already been cut, you will have to strip 1/2 inch of insulation from the end of each wire.)

Inside the converter are four screw terminals, color-coded to match the four colored wires inside the telephone line cord. Insert each wire into a screw-terminal slot of the same color in the converter and tighten the terminal screws. The phone can then be plugged into any modular outlet.

Replacing a hard-wired all telephone

Tools: Screwdriver, Wire cutters or Scissors, Pencil, or Paper clip

Materials: Modular Jack for Wall Telephone (630B)

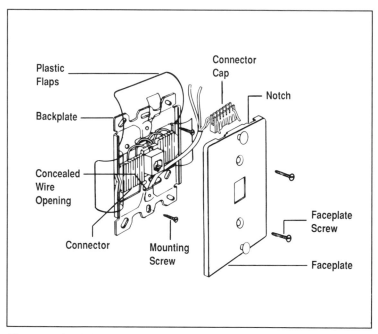

Figure 4-10 Wall Telephone Jack (630B)

There are many types of wall telephones, and you'll have to determine which kind you have before replacing it. This can be difficult to do without removing the telephone housing, since the housing usually conceals the connection. If you're not sure whether the phone is hard-wired, check the coiled handset cord; if it can be unplugged, the phone is probably modular and can be removed easily (see Chapter 3). If the handset cord is permanently attached, the telephone is hard-wired and must be replaced with a modular jack before a modular wall phone can be mounted.

First, remove the telephone housing. If your phone is one of the four types shown here, it should have a small U-shaped hole where the coiled handset cord enters the phone. Inside this hole is a tab that must be released to remove the housing. Using the eraser end of a pencil, push the tab up while pushing the bottom of the phone toward the wall with your other hand.

Other types of wall phones have screws to attach the housing. These screws are usually concealed beneath the small card that shows your telephone number. The clear plastic cover over the number card can be removed with a bent paper clip.

After the housing is removed, you should see a network of wires and screw terminals inside the telephone base that remains on the wall. Four of these wires must be cut to remove the phone. The wires to cut are the four color-coded conductors (red, green, yellow, black) that enter the phone from the telephone station wire in or on the wall. If you can't tell which wires to cut, you may have to unscrew the telephone base from the wall to identify the station wire (either in or on the wall) and follow its path into the phone to the four screw terminals. *(Continued)*

Caution: Be careful when cutting wires to remove a wall telephone. In some homes the station wire is routed to the phone from inside a hollow wall, and care must be taken so that the wire does not fall down into the wall after it is cut. A simple way to prevent this from happening is to attach the wire to a long piece of string. Tie the end of the string to an object nearby and attach it to the first one or two wires you cut. If the station wire falls down into the wall when the last wire is cut, you can use the string to retrieve it.

After the wires are cut, you can remove the telephone base from the wall by unscrewing the two screws used to mount it. The new modular jack can then be installed.

The first step is to mount the backplate. Both wood screws and anchor screws are provided so it can be mounted on a stud or on a hollow wall. Stud mounting is preferred, since it provides the most secure support for the phone.

Next, attach the four wires you cut earlier to the plastic connector caps provided. No wire stripping is necessary; just insert the wires into grooves in the connector caps, then push the caps onto the connectors as shown so that each wire is positioned to match the color of the wires built into the jack. Use a screwdriver as a lever to push the caps up as far as they will go.

Four extra slots in the connector are provided to connect a second station wire, which can be used to install an additional modular jack in another location as described in Chapters 5 and 6.

Two useful accessories for wall phones are described in Chapter 3. The **Dual Outlet Adapter** (733A) plugs into any modular jack for a wall phone and allows you to attach a second modular phone, answering machine, or other accessory to the same jack. For a more attractive appearance, a **Backboard** can be used to conceal any wall discoloration revealed when an older wall phone is replaced with a smaller one.

5 Home telephone wiring

This chapter describes several methods of routing and connecting telephone wiring to help you install a system of modular jacks. The home wiring products described in this chapter are designed to make almost any wiring job easier, and step-by-step installation instructions are included with each. Most home telephone wiring can be done quickly and inexpensively with a few home maintenance tools. However, before you install any wiring, make sure you are aware of all telephone regulations that apply in your area.

Planning your wiring routes

This chapter provides valuable tips to help you whether you want to add one outlet, extend your existing system, or completely rewire your home. However, to avoid wasted time, effort and materials, take a few minutes to plan the most efficient wiring routes for your home. First, consider which of the following wiring plans best meets your needs. There are two basic ways to wire your home, and each has distinct advantages.

Loop wiring is a simple way to connect many telephone outlets together on one wiring circuit. The advantage of this system is quick, easy installation. Loop wiring is best for apartments and houses smaller than 3,000 square feet, or for homes with only modest telephone requirements. In an **open loop** wiring plan, the wiring begins at the network interface (or at a wire junction connected to it) and runs from jack to jack throughout the home. In a **closed-loop** wiring plan, an extra wire path provides a more secure and reliable system. (See Figure 5-1.)

Home-run wiring is a method of connecting each telephone jack to a common point (usually a wire junction at or near the network interface). This system is suggested for larger homes, and for homes in which an office is installed or planned.

Home-run wiring requires more time and hardware to install,

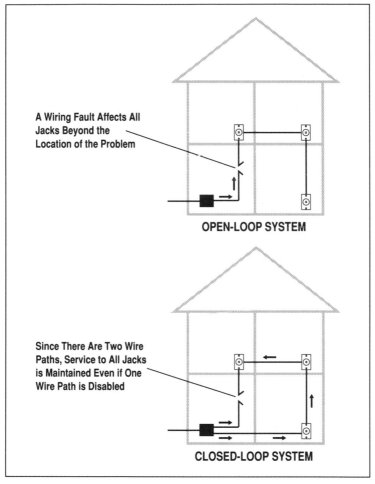

A Wiring Fault Affects All Jacks Beyond the Location of the Problem

OPEN-LOOP SYSTEM

Since There Are Two Wire Paths, Service to All Jacks is Maintained Even if One Wire Path is Disabled

CLOSED-LOOP SYSTEM

Figure 5-1 Loop wiring

but provides several advantages. If a wire is broken or shorted, for instance, the damage is confined to one room; the problem can be quickly identified and repaired. The reliability of home-run wiring is preferred in homes with telephone-linked energy management devices and security systems such as fire, medical, or intrusion alarms. In addition, this type of wiring can easily be upgraded for more complex communications needs such as an intercom, a

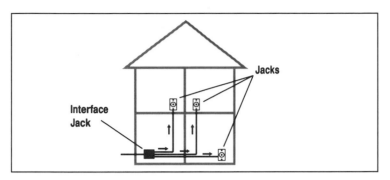

Figure 5-2 Home-run wiring

facsimile machine, a multi-line telephone system, or a computer system for personal or small-business use. (See Figure 5-2.)

For many homes, a **loop/home-run combination** is a practical alternative to a full home-run wiring system. Important data and security devices are connected directly to the wire junction nearest the interface, with other jacks attached either in a loop circuit or branching out from a second junction.

Safety instructions

Please read the important safety instructions on page 1 before beginning work on any wiring project described in this chapter.

Wiring guidelines

To assure a safe and reliable system of telephone wiring, take a few moments to read over the following suggestions.

1 Always use high-quality materials. We recommend using only AT&T telephone wire and wiring products.

2 Planning is made easier by sketching out a floor plan of your home showing where each jack will be installed. Make a list of the tools and materials you'll need, and estimate how much wiring will be required. Try to choose the straightest, most direct wire routes. When planning your wiring system, remember that jacks should be installed no farther than 200 feet from the point where wiring first enters your home.

3 Avoid installing wire in damp locations, or in places where the
   wire may come in contact with hot surfaces such as steam
   pipes, heating ducts, or hot water pipes.

4 Protect wiring from abrasion and possible damage. Do not route
   wire where it might be crimped or broken, such as through
   window or door openings. Never route loose or unprotected
   wire across stairwells, door openings, carpet walkways or other
   open spaces where it could present a tripping hazard. For a safer
   and more attractive installation, route wiring along the top
   surface of baseboards, the bottom surface of wainscoting and
   chair rails, beneath carpet edges, or in other protected locations.
   Always install wiring in accordance with the instructions
   beginning on page 1.

5 Never splice telephone wire. Splicing can cause noise and other
   problems in telephone wiring. Unless specifically directed to do
   so, never strip the color-coded insulation from the conductors
   inside station wire. Special terminals in most AT&T home
   wiring products allow wire to be connected quickly and easily
   without stripping or splicing.

6 Provide adequate support for wiring. Use fasteners that do not
   puncture or abrade wire insulation, and space them closely
   enough to support the wire securely. Check the recommended
   spacing chart guidelines before installing wire fasteners.

Recommended spacing for wire fasteners

	HORIZONTAL SPACING	VERTICAL SPACING	FROM CORNERS
Wire clamps or clips	16 inches	16 inches	2 inches
Wire staples	7 inches	7 inches	2 inches
Bridle rings	4 feet	—	2 to 8 in.
Drive rings	4 feet	8 feet	2 to 8 in.

Figure 5-3

Minimum telephone
wire separation

TYPE OF WIRING	MINIMUM SEPARATION	MINIMUM ALTERNATIVES
Bare electric light wiring or electric power wire of any kind (wire with no insulation)	5 feet	No alternatives
Single-conductor insulated wire (not more than 300 volts)	2 inches	See Note 1
Wire in conduit, in armored or non-metallic sheath cable, or power ground wires	None	—
Radio or television antenna lead-in or ground wires	4 inches	See Note 1
Signal or control wires	None	—
Cable-TV wiring (coaxial cable with grounded shielding)	None	—
Telephone drop wire (wire entering house from telephone pole or other distibution point) ...if protector is fused	2 inches	See Note 1
...if protector is not fused or if no protector required	None	—
Neon signs and other wiring associated with transformer	6 inches	No alternatives
Lightning rods or wires	6 feet	See Note 2

Note 1: If minimum separations cannot be maintained, enclose wiring in a plastic tube, wire guard or two layers of vinyl tape extending two inches beyond the point where telephone wiring crosses the other wire.

Note 2: Less than 6 feet of separation is acceptable if telephone, power and lightning-rod grounds are all connected to a common metallic cold-water pipe that is properly grounded; or if separately driven ground rods are used for telephone, power and lightning rods, and the rods are bonded together.

Figure 5-4

7 Isolate telephone wiring from electrical wiring and other possible sources of interference. Try to keep telephone wiring well away from electrical outlets. Never install telephone wires in a conduit or junction box with electrical wiring. If you must route telephone wiring across or parallel to any other kind of wiring, follow the guidelines in the Minimum Telephone Wire Separation chart on page 43.

8 Special care must be taken when installing any telephone wiring in recreational trailers, mobile homes and metal-sided buildings to ensure that any conducting surface is properly grounded. If you have any doubts, contact your local telephone company or an electrical contractor for advice.

9 After installing any new jacks or wiring, conduct the tests described in Chapter 7 to make sure everything has been connected correctly.

Types of telephone wire

There are two basic kinds of telephone wiring. Line cord is a flat, four-conductor cord usually used to connect a telephone or other accessory to a modular jack. Although line cord can be used to create a temporary modular jack (by plugging a 25-foot extension cord into an existing jack), it is not recommended for more extensive wiring.

Telephone wire, available in 50-foot lengths wherever AT&T wiring products are sold, is designed for home telephone wiring. It is intended for permanent indoor installation and should never be used outdoors, or as a substitute for telephone line cord.

There are several types of wire, but the most commonly used for home telephone wiring is called **D-station wire**, which contains four conducting wires, each sheathed in color-coded insulation for easy recognition.

A telephone circuit requires at least two wires. In a typical installation, only one pair of wires is used for basic telephone service; the others can be used for grounding, to connect a second phone line, to carry current for a lighted phone, or as spares if a problem develops in the pair used for basic telephone service.

The pair of wires used for basic telephone service consists of a "tip" wire (usually green) and a "ring" wire (usually red), terms

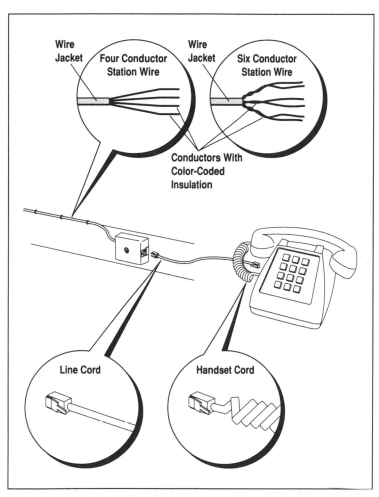

Figure 5-5 Examples of telephone wiring

which designate how each wire is used to carry telephone signals. It is very important that you maintain the continuity of this color-coding throughout all the wiring in your home. **Always connect red to red, and green to green**. Follow the instructions provided when connecting station wire to any telephone product, and never insert more than one color-coded conductor in each slot of a screw terminal or connecting cap.

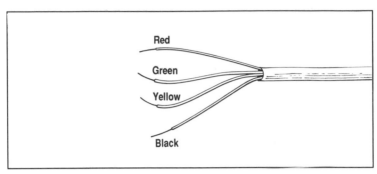

Figure 5-6 D-Station wire

In some homes, three-pair station wire may be already installed. This is similar to the D-station wire described above except that the cable contains six conductors instead of four, and a different color coding is used. When adding new wiring in homes with three-pair wire already installed, consult the wire coding chart to make sure you connect the wires correctly.

Station wire color coding

STANDARD COLORS	VARIATION A	VARIATION B	VARIATION C
Red	Blue (white bands)	Blue (white bands)	Blue
Green	White (blue bands)	White (blue bands)	White (blue bands)
Yellow	Orange (white bands)	Orange (white bands)	Orange
Black	White (orange bands)	White (orange bands)	White (orange bands)
	Green (white bands)		
	White (green bands)		

Note: "bands" refer to thin stripes of color on wire insulation

Figure 5-7

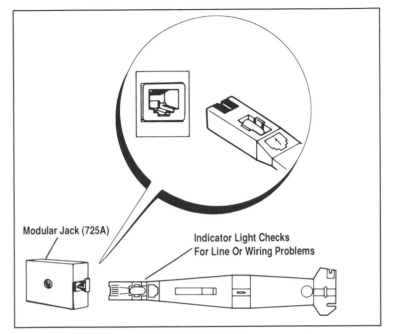

Figure 5-8 Telephone Line Tester

Use the right tool for the job

The **Telephone Line Tester** with slitter (953B) is an inexpensive tool that can simplify many installation jobs and greatly reduce the possibility of accidental damage to telephone wiring and components. This versatile tool can be used to strip wire insulation, to break out wire-channel tabs in modular jacks and junctions, and to install telephone wire conductors in many telephone products.

The line tester can also be used to check any wiring job before installing telephones, and can help avoid the expense of a service call if you don't have a second telephone to verify whether a problem is in your telephone or in your wiring. Potential problems can be detected quickly by plugging the tester into a modular jack for an instant reading of four important line conditions:

1 Tip and ring polarity: Indicates whether red and green telephone wire conductors have been reversed anywhere in the circuit.

2 Yellow and black wire polarity: Indicates whether yellow and black conductors have been reversed anywhere in the circuit.

3 Bad wire contacts: Indicates whether any wires in the circuit are loose or disconnected.

4 Electrical voltage on line: Detects the presence of AC voltage generated by a transformer used for speakerphones or telephones with lighted dials.

Installing a common connecting point

The starting place for any wiring in your home should be the network interface (see page 3). The first step in your wiring should be to connect a wire junction to the interface to function as a **common connecting point** for all the wiring in your home. This provides a convenient way to disconnect your entire telephone wiring system while making repairs or installing additional wiring.

First, mount a **Wire Junction** (742B) on a wall or baseboard near the interface. (See Figure 5-9.) Inside the junction are four sets of terminals. Three of them can be used to route station wires from

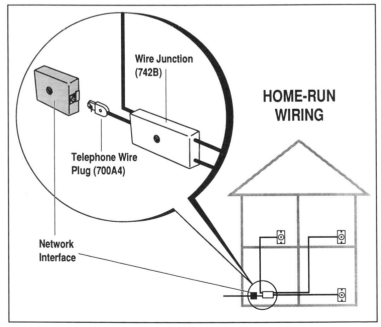

Figure 5-9 Installing a Wire Junction

the junction to connect jacks or additional wire junctions in other parts of your home. To the fourth set of terminals, attach a short length of telephone wire just slightly longer than necessary to reach the network interface. Install a **Telephone Wire Plug** (700A4) on the other end of the short telephone wire. This wire can then be plugged into your network interface. When it is unplugged, your wiring will be safely disconnected from the network while you work.

A quick alternative to a wire junction connecting point

To install a basic loop system, you might prefer to run telephone wire directly from your network interface instead of installing a wire junction. (See Figure 5-10.) A simple way to do this is to connect a **Telephone Wire Plug** (700A4) to one end of the telephone wire. This wire can then be plugged into your network interface and routed to the first jack you want to install. From that jack you can route additional wire to the next jack, and so on.

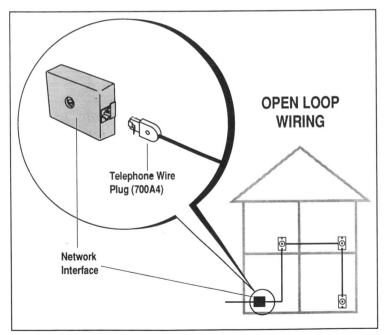

OPEN LOOP
WIRING

Telephone Wire
Plug (700A4)

Network
Interface

Figure 5-10 Basic loop system

Although this kind of **open-loop** system can be installed quickly, it provides only one wire path. Therefore, telephone service to every jack in the home depends on the same wire path. If a problem were to develop anywhere in the wiring, all phones beyond the wiring fault would be out of service until the problem could be identified and corrected.

A **closed-loop** system provides a measure of protection against such problems. To close the loop, connect an additional wire to the last jack in the system and route it back to the network interface. (See Figure 5-11.) In effect, this is like having a backup wiring system in place, since it provides two wire paths to each jack.

Installing a closed-loop system is easiest if a wire junction is connected to the interface. If you don't install a junction, an alternative method is to run a length of station wire from the last jack in the system back to the interface and attach a second Telephone Wire Plug to the end of the wire. With a **Dual Outlet Adapter** (267A2), you can plug both wire routes into the interface

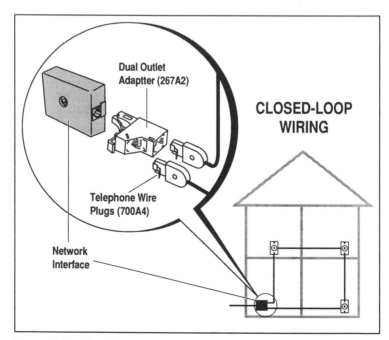

Figure 5-11 Closed loop system

jack. Remember, though, that you'll have to unplug the adapter from the interface to disconnect your wiring completely from the network while working.

Using wire junctions to extend your wiring system

Additional wire junctions can be installed in other locations and used to route new wiring throughout your home. A wire junction can be installed up to 50 feet from its point of connection. Up to three telephone wires can be routed from each junction to connect jacks or additional wire junctions to branch circuits out to other parts of your home. (See Figure 5-12.)

Special screw terminals inside the junction allow you to connect station wire quickly and easily. No wire stripping is necessary; the conductors fit into slots that pierce the wire insulation and make secure connections when the terminals are tightened with a screw-driver.

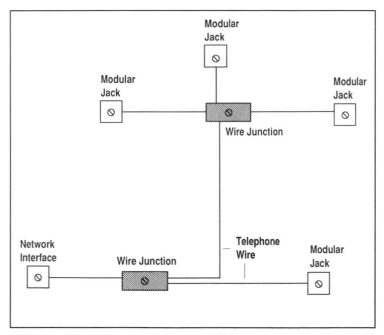

Figure 5-12 Each wire junction can connect as may as 3 jacks

Extending new wiring from an existing jack or junction

The simplest way to extend your modular system is to route new telephone wire from an existing jack or wire junction. The new wire can be easily connected to any modular jack or wire junction because they contain special terminals that require no wire stripping. (See Figure 5-13.)

Inside wire junctions and jacks are four screw terminals, each color-coded to match the color of wire conductors. Use a screwdriver to loosen each screw about three turns. If you have a **Telephone Line Tester** (953B), use its wire slitter to remove three inches of the outer jacket of the station wire to expose the color-coded conductors.

Insert each conductor into a vacant slot in the appropriate terminal, push it all the way through until about 1/4-inch emerges on the other side, then screw the terminals down tightly so the insulation is pierced. If you are working with a wire junction or surface-mounted jack, it may be necessary to break out one of the four wire channels to create an opening for the wire before you replace the cover. A notch in the line tester is provided for this purpose.

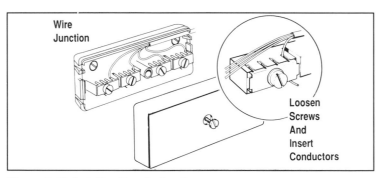

Figure 5-13 Installing the wire junction

Extending new wiring from an existing wall telephone

Jacks for wall telephones use a connector different from the screw terminals found in standard modular jacks. After removing the faceplate, fold back the clear plastic flaps to expose two wire connectors, one on each side of the jack. Attached to the bottom of each connector is a beige plastic cap; pull each cap down to remove it. (See Figure 5-14.)

Inside each cap are wire slots color-coded to match the color of the wire insulation. Two slots are provided for each color. Strip three inches from the outer jacket of the station wire and insert each of the four colored conductors into one of the vacant slots marked with the same color as the wire.

When you replace the caps on the connectors, make sure the caps are positioned correctly to match the colors of the wires in the connectors. Use a screwdriver as a lever to push each cap all the way up so it is connected securely. Finally, route the wire through one of the slots provided, fold the plastic flaps back over the connectors, and replace the faceplate.

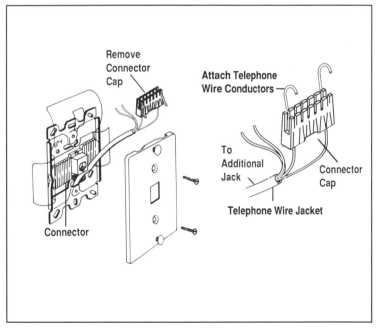

Figure 5-14 Extending new wiring from an existing wall telephone

Tapping into an existing station wire

If there is no jack or junction near a location where you want to install new wiring, there may be an existing station wire nearby that can be used as the starting point for a new wire route. Often you can find an existing wire on a baseboard, in a closet or cabinet, or attached to joists in an attic or basement. Check carefully to make sure you identify the correct wire; a beige doorbell wire or meter-reading wire may sometimes resemble telephone wire.

Once you have found the correct wire, examine it to see whether any slack exists. If there is no slack in the line, it is often possible to remove a few fasteners and stretch the wire slightly. (Pull gently, however; telephone wire is not as strong as electrical wire.) If you can obtain at least three inches of slack in the wire, it can be cut and attached either to a modular jack or to a wire junction as described on page 52. Additional telephone wire can then be routed from the new jack or junction to another location.

If no slack can be gained, an alternative is to cut the wire and install two wire junctions (or a jack and a junction) at least two inches apart. Each end of the cut wire can be attached to a junction, and the junctions then bridged with a separate length of wire.

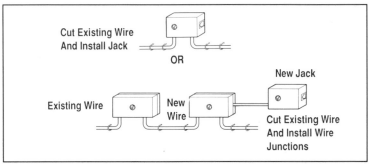

Figure 5-15 Tapping into existing telephone wire

NOTE: Older types of telephone wire may be found in some homes. Be especially careful when working with older wire, since the insulation of the conductors may not be color-coded. In some older wire, the tip and ring conductors are identified by a colored silk thread bound inside the insulation next to each conductor. Also, since its insulation is thicker, the conductors of older wires often must be stripped before they can be attached to terminals in a modular jack or junction. Use a single-edge razor blade or a sharp knife to remove 1/2 inch of insulation from each conductor, being careful not to nick the wire.

Installing exposed wiring

Installing telephone wire along the surface of a wall requires few tools, and usually can be done more quickly than routing wires inside walls. In many cases the entire job can be completed in minutes, using only a screwdriver.

When installing exposed wire, try to choose routes where the wire will be inconspicuous and well protected. Run wire inside cabinets and closets, or beneath shelving wherever possible. In paneled rooms, wiring can often be concealed under panels or beneath hollow corner trim or baseboard molding. Where wiring must be installed on an exposed wall, route it along baseboards, door and window frames, picture molding or chair rails. Take up all slack and secure the wire well, so it cannot present a tripping hazard.

A recommended method is to run wiring along the top of baseboards using **Telephone Wire Clips**. (See Figure 5-16.) Only thumb or screwdriver pressure is needed to insert clips between the

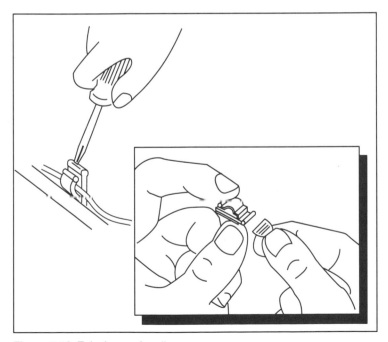

Figure 5-16 Telephone wire clip

baseboard and the wall. Wire clips also include an adhesive pad that can be used to fasten wire to most smooth surfaces. Whichever method you use, space clips along the wire at intervals no greater than 16 inches. Round corners by bending the wire in a gentle curve, and install a clip on each wall two inches from the corner.

Another method is to conceal wiring beneath carpeting where the carpet meets the wall. If the carpet edges are tacked to the floor, it may be necessary to remove tacks with pliers or a screwdriver tip so the carpet edge can be lifted. If the carpet is attached with a tack strip, use pliers to pull the carpet free. When laying wire under a carpet, avoid high-traffic areas, and be careful to place the wire so its insulation is not punctured by tacks (or a tack strip) when you reattach the carpet to the floor.

Where wiring must be routed around doors and windows, wire clips can be inserted under door frames or window molding. Route wire around door frames rather than running it across a doorway on the floor. Where wire must span a doorway, cover it with a metal door sill or carpet sealing strip.

Routing wire through walls

If you take proper precautions, drilling through a wall is often the easiest way to route a wire into another room. In homes with typical plasterboard interior walls, this is usually a simple job. You will need only a drill with a 1/4-inch bit (at least six inches long) and a plastic soda straw.

The following guidelines will help you determine how and where to drill holes for telephone wire.

1 When drilling through a wall, be careful to avoid hidden pipes, ducts or wiring. Never drill near an electrical outlet.

2 Determine the wall thickness and composition before drilling. Plasterboard walls are usually 4 1/2 inches thick, but in older homes the walls may be much thicker. A carbide-tip bit should be used to drill through masonry walls.

3 Drill just above the baseboard, at least five inches from any door or window openings. Sound the wall by tapping to locate studs and cross-braces. Tap the wall lightly with a screwdriver handle wrapped in clean cloth, and drill where the wall sounds hollow.

4 Since telephone wire is limp and difficult to insert through holes in both sides of a hollow wall, push a soda straw through first, then insert the wire through the straw. (See Figure 5-17.) If you still have difficulty, push a length of coat-hanger wire through the wall first, insert the straw over it, then remove the coat hanger and push the station wire through. (See Figure 5-18.) For a more finished appearance, the holes can be sealed with putty or quick-setting plaster and painted over after the wire has been installed.

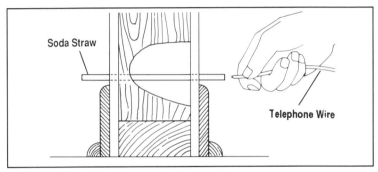

Figure 5-17 Inserting telephone wire through a hollow wall

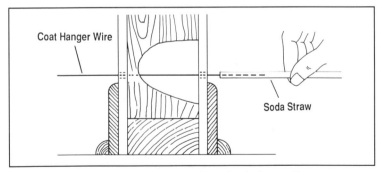

Figure 5-18 Inserting telephone wire through a hollow wall

Installing wire in basements and attics

In many cases, routing wiring beneath a floor or above a ceiling is a more efficient way to wire your home. And since less wiring is exposed, the installation is more attractive.

The choice of attic or basement wiring often depends on where the telephone wire first enters your home. In one-story homes it is usually most convenient to install a common connecting point and all wire junctions on the same level. In an attic, for example, you can install one or more junctions on ceiling joists and route the wire from each junction down through the ceiling to jacks in each room. Another aspect to consider is wall insulation. If you must run wiring inside insulated walls it may be easier to take the shorter route up from a basement than a longer route down from the attic.

When installing wire in an attic or basement, use staples or wire clamps to route it along joists or beams whenever possible instead of spanning from joist to joist. If you must span joists, install wiring no more than three inches from a wall and secure it with fasteners on each joist. Use conduit when available (or when required by local building codes), but never place both electrical and telephone wires in the same conduit.

Routing wire from floor to floor

There are several methods of routing wire from an attic or basement, or from floor to floor. The simplest way is to drill directly through a ceiling or floor where two walls meet, then run the wire in the corner to a jack installed on a baseboard. If you are routing wire down from the attic, you can conceal the wire by choosing a corner that is inside a closet or cabinet, or by covering the exposed wire with inside corner molding.

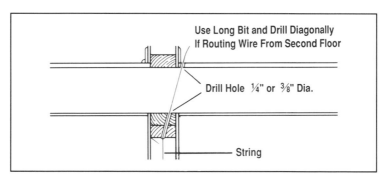

Figure 5-19 Routing wire from second floor

Routing wire inside walls

A much better, but more difficult, method is to run wiring inside hollow walls to the jack. First you must find a suitable location to run the wire through the wall. To run wire down from the ceiling, the wall must be hollow from top to bottom. Sound the wall by tapping to find a location between studs with no cross-bracing to block the wire path. Avoid walls containing electrical wires.

Generally, interior walls are more suitable for routing wire. Exterior walls more often contain obstacles such as cross-bracing and insulation, and may be difficult to reach from the attic because of the roof slope. If you must route wire in an exterior wall, keep well clear of corners since cross-bracing is often installed where outside bearing walls meet.

The next step involves a procedure known as "fishing" the wire. (See Figure 5-20.) If routing wire down from the ceiling, you'll need an extra-long drill bit (1/4-inch to 3/8-inch diameter) to drill a hole through the top plate of the wall. Drill another hole through the wall just above the baseboard and directly below the first hole. Fasten a weight to a strong string and drop the weighted string down inside the wall to the floor. A length of stiff coat-hanger wire

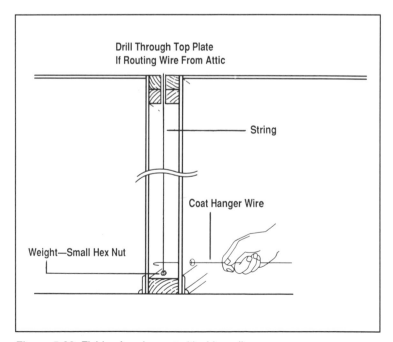

Figure 5-20 Fishing for wire routed inside walls

bent into a fishhook shape can be used to snare the string and pull it out through the lower hole. If you have difficulty snaring the string, have someone in the attic move the string around until it is in a better position.

Finally, tie the string securely to the telephone wire and wrap the knot with tape to prevent it from being snagged inside the wall. Then, from the attic, pull the string through the lower hole and up through the wall until the wire emerges in the attic.

The procedure for routing wire up from a basement or crawl space is similar except that the weighted string is lowered from a hole drilled above the baseboard and "fished" from the basement, through a hole drilled in the bottom plate of the wall.

Routing wire through a pipe partition

If you have difficulty finding a suitable place to route wire through a wall, a pipe partition may be a useful alternative. A bathroom soil pipe, usually concealed in a wall just behind the toilet, usually offers the best passage since a clear space often surrounds the pipe from the basement to the roof. A cold-water pipe may also provide a clear passage but could be a poor choice since it often sweats in the summer, and usually shares the same partition with a hot-water pipe. Never route wiring near heating ducts or near pipes containing hot water, gas or steam.

Exterior wiring

Any wiring installed outside your home requires special materials and installation procedures for protection. In addition, local regulations often restrict or prohibit the installation of exterior wiring. We recommend that you check with your local telephone company before attempting the installation of any outdoor wiring or equipment other than the outdoor modular jack described in Chapter 6.

6 Installing modular jacks

This chapter describes the many different kinds of modular jacks you can install to extend your home telephone system. Although detailed, step-by-step instructions are included with each AT&T modular jack, this chapter will explain many useful installation guidelines and help you decide which jacks are best suited for each location in your home.

All AT&T modular jacks are designed to be installed quickly and easily; most installation jobs described in this chapter can be completed in a few minutes using only a screwdriver. However, if you haven't already done so, take a few minutes to read Chapter 1 and make sure you are aware of any local restrictions before you begin.

Planning modular jack locations

The number and location of jacks you install will be determined by several factors. In the past, a general rule of thumb was to install a jack for a wall telephone in the kitchen and a standard modular jack in the living room, the family room and in each bedroom. However, the growing popularity of answering systems, personal computers, fax machines, security systems and other telephone-related conveniences has made the installation of two jacks in many rooms a more practical idea.

Many new homes have an extra jack in each bedroom and in all large or frequently used rooms such as libraries, dens and family or living rooms. Even if only one is used regularly, the installation of two modular jacks in many rooms allows quick relocation of telephones and can eliminate the need for extension cords and extra wiring later if redecoration or furniture rearrangement makes one jack inaccessible.

Choose the right jack for each location. Three things are important to consider when choosing the type of jack: appearance, protection and convenience. **Flush-mounted jacks**, which mount inside hollow walls, are recommended for exposed areas where appearance is important. Jacks for **wall telephones** are typically installed in high-activity areas or in locations where surface space for a desk telephone is limited such as in kitchens, bathrooms, utility rooms, garages and workshops. For often-used outdoor areas such as a patio, porch or balcony, a special **weatherproof jack** is available for extra protection against dust and moisture.

When assessing your telephone requirements, keep in mind future as well as present needs. If you plan to add conveniences later — such as a second telephone line, a fax machine, an inter-com, a security system, a computer system, or a telephone-linked energy management system — you may want to add more jacks now to anticipate later expansion. Don't neglect areas of your home that may later be converted to an office, living space, or work area such as a basement, attic, or garage.

Safety instructions

Please read the important safety instructions beginning on page 1 before installing jacks or working with any telephone products other than those that simply plug into an existing modular jack.

Jack installation guidelines

To assure reliable service from your home telephone system, you should take a few minutes to read over the following sugges-tions.

1 Always use high-quality products. We recommend using only AT&T modular jacks.

2 Plan your jack locations carefully before you begin. Try to choose convenient, easily accessible places to install jacks where they will be well protected. Keep jacks well away from electrical outlets. Remember that jacks should be installed no farther than 200 feet from the point where wiring first enters your home.

3 Always read the installation instructions provided with each jack, and make sure all color-coded wires are attached to the correct terminal. Special wire terminals built into all AT&T jacks allow you to connect one additional station wire to extend

your telephone system. Never insert more than one conductor into each slot of a terminal.

4 Never install telephone jacks in locations that would permit someone to use a telephone near a bath tub, laundry tub, wash bowl, kitchen sink, swimming pool, or in wet areas such as a damp basement.

5 Jacks installed in a kitchen should be located a reasonable distance from grounded surfaces such as sinks, refrigerators and ranges.

6 After installing any new jack, conduct the tests described in Chapter 7 to make sure it has been connected correctly.

Installing surface-mounted jacks

Tools: Screwdriver
Telephone Line Tester with Slitter (953B)

Materials: Modular Jack (725A)

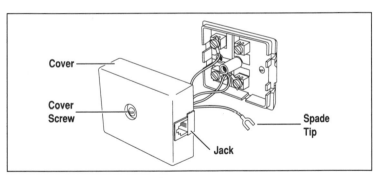

Figure 6-1 Modular Jack (725A)

The jack shown here can be installed quickly and easily on the surface of a baseboard, wall or cabinet.

To install the jack on a wall, mount it at the same height as electrical outlets for a better appearance. In damp locations, a mounting height of 18 inches above the floor is recommended. Two wood screws are provided for baseboard mounting; anchor screws should be used if the jack is mounted on a hollow wall.

After mounting the jack base on the wall, loosen the four screw terminals about three turns. Use a wire slitter to remove three inches of insulation from the outer jacket of the telephone wire. Insert each of the four color-coded conductors into a vacant slot beneath the appropriate screw terminal and tighten the screws. Finally, break out one of the wire-channel tabs, insert the telephone wire, and screw the cover onto the base, making sure no wires are pinched when the cover is attached.

Installing a flush-mounted jack

Tools: Pliers
            Screwdriver
            Keyhole or sabre saw
            Drill with 1/4-inch bit
            Telephone Line Tester with Slitter (953B)

Materials: Modular Jack, Flush Mounted (725E)
            Pencil
            Weighted string
            Coat hanger or other stiff wire

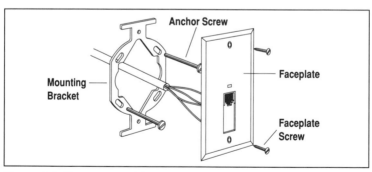

Figure 6-2 Flush-mounted Jack (725E)

Flush-mounted jacks take slightly longer to install, but are much more attractive than surface-mounted jacks when properly mounted.

First, choose a suitable place to install the jack that is well away from electrical outlets. Choose a location where no pipes or wiring conduits are concealed inside the wall that may be harmed by drilling. Plan to mount the jack so that it matches the height of existing electrical outlets. In damp locations, mount it at least 18 inches above the floor. Sound the wall by tapping to find a suitable point about midway between studs.

To install the jack you'll have to cut a hole in the wall. A mounting bracket provided with the jack can be used as a template to mark the hole position and anchor-screw locations on the wall with a pencil. After the hole is cut, drill two 1/4-inch holes above and below it as shown to install the bracket with anchor screws. Make sure the bracket is installed straight, on a true vertical line.

The next step depends on how you've routed your telephone wire. If you plan to run wiring to the jack from an attic or basement, read the description on page 56 for suggestions on routing the wire inside the wall. If your telephone wire runs along the surface of the wall on a baseboard, you may want to use an alternative method of "fishing" the wire through the wall.

To run baseboard-mounted wire to the jack, first drill a 1/4-inch hole just above the baseboard, directly beneath the jack position. Drop the weighted string down through the hole you've cut for the jack. Use pliers to bend a stiff wire into a fishhook shape, insert it through the 1/4-inch hole below, and snare the string to pull a loop through the lower hole. The telephone wire can then be tied to the string and drawn up through the hole you've cut for the jack.

Connect the color-coded conductors to vacant slots in the screw terminals as described in the section above and attach the jack faceplate with two screws provided. For a more finished appearance, you may want to seal the lower hole with putty or a quick-setting plaster.

Installing a jack for a wall telephone

Tools: Screwdriver
Drill with 1/4-inch bit
Telephone Line Tester with Slitter (953B)

Materials: Modular Jack for Wall Telephone (630B)

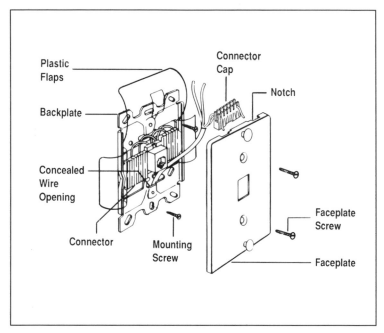

Figure 6-3 Wall Telephone Jack (630B)

    There are several ways to install a jack for a wall-mounted modular telephone. To replace a non-modular wall phone, see page 36. If a modular jack already exists in the room, a Phonemount can be quickly installed as described on page 22. The standard wall-phone jack described here takes longer to install, but is often a better choice for two reasons: It can be installed in rooms where there is no existing jack, and it presents a more attractive appearance since telephone wire can be more easily concealed than the Phonemount line cord.

The jack can be mounted on a stud or a hollow wall, though stud mounting is preferred since it provides the most secure support for the phone. If the jack is installed in a paneled room, one alternative is to mount it on a furring strip; these are two- to three-inch wood strips often found under the edges of panels. If no suitable location over a stud or furring strip can be found, use the anchor screws provided to mount the jack on a hollow wall.

Use the mounting bracket provided as a template to mark the wall at the position of the mounting screws, so that the lower screw is 48 to 52 inches from the floor. Make sure the bracket is straight, then mark the mounting screw positions, drill a 1/4-inch hole for each screw, and mount the bracket. If you are mounting the jack on a stud, use a smaller bit to drill through the wallboard and into the stud a short distance to create a starter hole for the wood screws.

To conceal the telephone wire, it can be routed through the wall from an attic or basement as described on page 56, or along the baseboard as shown on page 55. An alternative method is to run the wire along the wall and into the jack through a notch provided in the bottom of the faceplate.

After removing the faceplate, fold back the clear plastic flaps to expose two wire connectors, one on each side of the jack. Attached to the bottom of each connector is a beige plastic cap; pull each cap down to remove it.

Inside each cap are wire slots color-coded to match the color of the wire insulation. Two slots are provided for each color. Strip three inches from the outer jacket of the station wire and insert each of the four colored conductors into one of the vacant slots marked with the same color as the wire.

When you replace the caps on the connectors, make sure the caps are positioned correctly to match the colors of the wires in the connectors. Use a screwdriver as a lever to push each cap all the way up so it is connected securely. Finally, route the wire through one of the slots provided, fold the plastic flaps back over the connectors, and replace the faceplate.

Add-a-jack kit

Tools: Screwdriver
            Hammer

Materials: Add-a-Jack Kit (for wall telephones; for table phones)

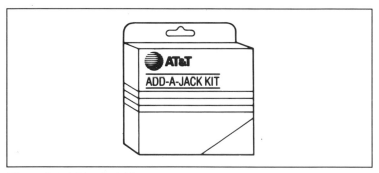

Figure 6-4 Add-a-Jack Kit

The convenient **Add-a-Jack kit** contains everything you need
to install an additional jack. The kit is available in two versions.
One contains a baseboard jack for use with table telephones, the
other contains a jack with mounting studs for use with wall
telephones. Both kits also include a Dual Outlet Adapter, 50 feet of
wire and all mounting hardware. Installation is simple and quick,
usually requiring only a screwdriver, a hammer, and the multi-
purpose installation tool provided with each kit. An illustrated
manual is also included to guide you step by step through the
installation.

Installing an outdoor jack

Tools: Screwdriver
Telephone Line Tester with Slitter (953B)
Drill with 1/4-inch bit
Bit extension if necessary

Materials: Outdoor Modular Jack (Z625WP4)
Coat hanger or other stiff wire
Caulking material

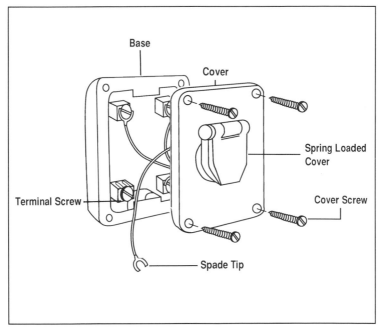

Figure 6-5 Outdoor Modular Jack (Z625WP4) (Gasket not shown)

This jack is designed to provide a durable and weatherproof connection in outdoor areas adjacent to the house such as a patio, porch or balcony. The jack should be mounted on a vertical surface such as an exterior wall of the house, preferably under a soffit, or roof overhang.

How wiring is routed to the jack will depend entirely on your home's construction and where the jack is located. In cases where wiring must pass through an exterior wall, check for any obstructions such as pipes or electrical conduits before drilling through the wall. Also check the thickness and composition of the wall to make sure you have a suitable drill bit capable of penetrating the wall.

Since telephone wire is limp and difficult to insert through several inches of an exterior wall, try pushing a length of coathanger wire through the hole first, then attach the wire and draw it through the wall. Make sure you leave enough slack to connect the wire to the jack. After the jack is installed, use a good caulking compound to seal the hole.

The base of the jack is mounted with wood screws or anchor screws, and the telephone wire is connected in the same way as a standard modular jack except that a grommet and gasket are used to seal the jack housing.

A special modular plug assembly provided with the jack connects to a telephone line cord to seal out dust and moisture when the telephone is plugged in. When the jack is not in use, the opening is sealed by a spring-loaded cap. The jack can be secured with a small padlock to protect against unauthorized use.

Note: Although the jack is weatherproof, remember that telephone wire is not intended for outdoor use. Special precautions must be taken to protect the wire if this jack is to be installed in a location away from the house that would require wiring to be exposed. In addition, since local regulations may restrict such wiring, we suggest contacting your local telephone company for advice before routing telephone wire from your house to another location.

Modular jacks for pre-wired homes

Tools: Screwdriver

Materials: Modular Jack,
Flush Mounted/Prewire (725H)
Modular Jack for Wall Telephone/Prewire (830A)
Faceplate/Prewire (65B)

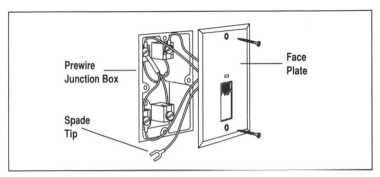

Figure 6-6 Prewire Flush Mounted Jack (725H)

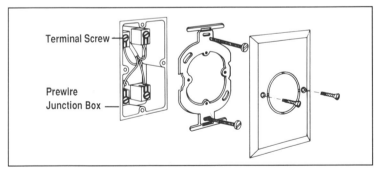

Figure 6-7 Prewire Faceplate (65B)

In newer homes, telephone wiring installed during construction is routed to junction boxes throughout the house. These pre-installed junction boxes are installed in the wall about 12 to 18 inches from the floor, and usually covered by blank plastic faceplates.

Remove the faceplates to determine how the junction boxes have been wired; if the wires are already attached to screw termi-

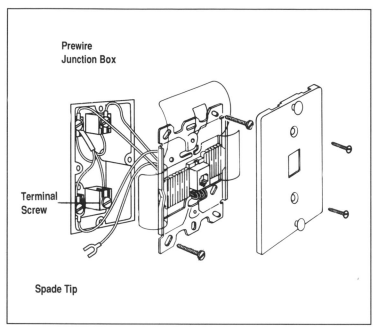

Figure 6-8 Prewire Wall Phone Jack (830A)

nals, special jacks (marked "Prewire" on the package) can be installed in minutes using only a screwdriver. Two types of prewire jacks are available; a flush-mounted modular jack, and a jack for wall telephones. Additional blank faceplates are also available to conceal unused junction boxes.

If your home has junction boxes without prewired screw terminals, flush jacks can be installed as described on page 64.

7 Testing and troubleshooting

After making any modifications to your home telephone system, you should conduct a simple test to make sure everything is working properly. The most reliable way to check your wiring installation is by using a **Telephone Line Tester** (953B). An alternate method is to use a telephone as described on page 75. When making adjustments to correct wiring problems, always follow the important safety instructions beginning on page 1.

When conducting the following tests, remember that red and green wires are usually used to provide basic telephone service. If you have two telephone lines in your home, the red and green wires are usually referred to as Line 1, and the yellow and black wires are used for Line 2. If the wires in your home have conductors with different colors, see the chart on page 46 to determine which colors correspond to the red, green, yellow and black wires described in this section.

Using a line tester

The **Telephone Line Tester** can be used to check any jack installation or wiring job before telephones are installed. You should conduct the following two tests after installing each component of your telephone wiring system. Before testing, make sure you have reconnected your home telephone wiring to the network interface.

Test 1: Line 1 Polarity

This test checks whether the red and green wires are connected correctly. Hold the tester so the "1" is opposite the notched side of the jack opening as shown. Plug the tester into the jack and check the small indicator light.

Green light = Wiring is good.

Red light = Wires are reversed. Disconnect the telephone

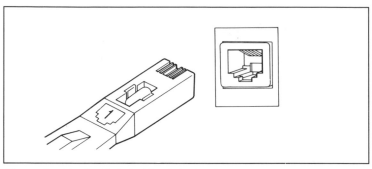

Figure 7-1 Testing Polarity-Line 1 (red and green wire)

circuit, open the jack, and reverse the red and green wire connections.

No light = Problem. Disconnect the circuit, open the jack, and check to make sure the red and green wires are firmly connected to wire terminals.

Test 2: Yellow and Black Wire (or Line 2) Polarity

This test checks whether the yellow and black wires are connected correctly. Turn the tester upside down (so that the "2" is opposite the notched side of the jack opening) plug it in, and check the indicator light.

Green light = Wiring is good.

Red light = Wires are reversed. Disconnect the telephone circuit, open the jack, and reverse the yellow and black wire connections.

Yellow light = AC voltage on the line. This condition is usually caused by a transformer required for some telephones that have lighted dials. If the transformer is not needed, it should be unplugged and removed.

No light = Disregard if you have only one telephone line. If you have a two-line system, no light indicates a problem. Disconnect the circuit, open the jack, and check to make sure the yellow and black wires are firmly connected to terminals.

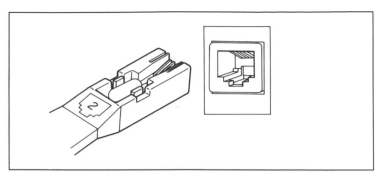

Figure 7-2 Testing Polarity-Line 2 (yellow and black wire)

Using a telephone to test your wiring

If you don't have a line tester, the following test can be performed using a working telephone.

Step 1: Check the telephone

To make sure the test telephone is working properly, plug it directly into the network interface and dial a number. If the telephone does not work properly, the test cannot be performed since a problem exists either in the telephone or in the telephone company wiring. If the telephone works normally, reconnect your wiring to the interface and perform Steps 2 and 3 for each jack in your home.

Step 2: Check for dial tone

Plug the telephone into the jack to be tested, lift the handset, and listen for a dial tone. If you hear nothing, you have a bad contact. Disconnect the circuit, open the jack, and check to make sure all wires are firmly connected to wire terminals.

Step 3: Check for tip and ring polarity

If you hear a dial tone, dial a telephone number. If you continue to hear a dial tone during and after dialing, the red and green wires are reversed. Disconnect the telephone circuit, open the jack, and reverse the red and green wire connections.

If you have two telephone lines and the same problem occurs on the second line, the yellow and black wires are reversed.

Problems and solutions

If you have a problem with your telephone system, try the following suggestions before seeking outside repair assistance. If you have difficulty with any AT&T home telephone wiring products, call the AT&T National Sales and Service Center at 1 800 222-3111. The call is toll-free, and we'll be glad to answer questions about any AT&T wiring products.

No dial tone

1 Try dialing a number. If nothing happens, make sure the telephone is working by plugging it into the network interface. If the telephone still doesn't work, try a second phone. If the second phone works, the first phone is defective. If neither phone works, the trouble is probably in the local telephone company line.

2 If you get a dial tone at the network interface but not at a jack, disconnect the system at the interface, open the jack, and check to make sure all wires are securely connected to wire terminals.

3 If no loose connections can be found, you may have a broken wire somewhere in the circuit. If practical, remove the wiring to the jack and replace it. If the wire cannot be removed, there are two other alternatives.

a) If you have an open-circuit loop system as shown on page 40 (if one station wire runs from jack to jack and connects all the telephones in your home to the interface), determine which jack is the last on the circuit. A new wire can be connected to the last jack and routed back to the interface (or common connecting point). This closes the loop, and provides service to all your phones.

b) If the disabled jack is wired directly to the network interface (as in the home-run system shown on page 41) an easier method is to switch to a spare set of conductors. Disconnect the red and green wires and substitute the yellow and black wire pair for telephone service to the jack. This can only be done, however, if the yellow and black wires are not being used for a second telephone line, or to carry electrical current for a lighted phone.

Dial tone continues when a number is dialed

Normally, the dial tone stops when the first digit of a telephone number is dialed. If you continue to hear a dial tone while you are dialing, the tip and ring wires may be reversed. Disconnect the system at the interface, open the jack, and reverse the red and green wire connections.

Noise on the telephone line

1 This problem could have several sources. The most common source of noise in home wiring is a loose connection in a jack or wire junction. Other causes could be dust, dirt or water fouling a connection. Check to make sure all wire connections are clean and tight, and that no wiring is exposed to water or sources of heat such as a hot water pipe or steam pipe.

2 Stress on wiring can cause intermittent noise if the wire is not completely broken. Check to see if any wiring is pinched or stretched too tightly around a sharp corner. If either condition exists, the wire probably has been damaged and should be replaced.

3 Another potential noise source is electrical interference. Make sure all telephone wires and jacks are installed well clear of any electrical wiring; check the chart on page 43 for guidelines on minimum separation of telephone wires from other types of wiring. A constant, low hum on the line could be caused by electrical interference, or by a false ground created when a bare wire comes in contact with a grounded metal surface. The problem could be abrasion that has worn insulation from a wire; if so the wire should be replaced.

4 If you have problems with radio signals, a special filter (described on page 26) may be used to suppress interference from nearby commercial radio stations.

8 Telephones and accessories

Once you have extended your home telephone system, you may want to add new telephones and accessories. This chapter gives a general description of some of the many high-quality, modular telephone products now available from AT&T. From basic telephones to the most advanced telecommunications equipment, all products described in this chapter are built to the same exacting standards of quality and reliability you expect from AT&T.

Basic telephones

Basic telephones are available in several models and colors. Each can be plugged into any modular jack for quick and easy installation, and all are hearing-aid compatible.

Traditional touch-tone telephones are available in table and wall-mounted models, both with adjustable electronic ringers. For added convenience, each is available with features such as last-number redial (one touch of a key redials the last number you called), a mute button (silences the phone so your caller can't hear you talking to someone else in the room) and a Dial Mode selector switch to allow complete compatibility with any type of telephone service.

Stylish Trimline® phones allow both pulse and tone dialing, and can be mounted on a wall or used as a desk telephone. Three different Trimline phones are available in six colors. Standard features include lighted dial buttons, receiver and ringer volume controls, last-number redial, and a mute button. The Trimline 220 remembers three high-priority telephone numbers that can be dialed with one touch of a button. The expanded memory of the more advanced Trimline 230 allows fast dialing of up to nine frequently called telephone numbers in addition to the three high-priority numbers that can be dialed with one touch.

Feature telephones

Many electronic telephones are now available with a built-in memory to store frequently called telephone numbers. Once you store a telephone number in memory, you can call it at any time simply by pressing one or two buttons.

Feature telephones are available that store as many as 32 frequently called numbers in memory. All models can store both local and long-distance numbers, and can be used with either pulse or tone-dialing service. Many models include such features as last-number redial and a mute button for privacy.

For additional security, some models are available with memory buttons for emergency numbers. In addition to storing other telephone numbers, these phones can store fire, police and medical emergency numbers in special memory locations. Any of the emergency numbers can be dialed instantly with one touch of a button. Power is provided by the telephone line, so most phones can be used even during electrical power failures.

More advanced models offer many other convenient features in addition to memory dialing. Some include a built-in timer and LCD display screen to show the date, time, telephone number and elapsed time of each call.

Cordless telephones

A variety of cordless telephones now available offer complete mobility without sacrificing sound quality. The base unit plugs into any modular jack and continuously recharges handset batteries while the handset remains on the base. The handset can be moved freely throughout the house or even outdoors to make and receive calls.

Many AT&T cordless phones include paging and intercom systems to allow communication between the handset and base unit, as well as security systems to protect against unauthorized use. More advanced models offer additional features such as digital security systems, extended range and battery life, automatic redialing and volume control, memory storage of frequently called numbers, mute and hold buttons, and speakerphone operation. Replacement parts and accessories for cordless telephones are described in Chapter 3.

Telephone answering systems

AT&T offers a wide variety of answering systems to meet any need. Basic systems offer one-touch playback of recorded messages and allow you to screen incoming calls; you can listen as your caller leaves a message, or pick up any extension phone on the same line to stop recording and talk to your caller.

Most models include a remote-control feature that allows you to call home from any other telephone and listen to your messages. These systems are available in "beeperless" models that can be operated simply by pressing the keys on any touch-tone telephone. Remote models also offer a "Toll-Saver" feature that allows you to check for messages and hang up without having to pay for the call if you have no messages waiting.

More advanced models allow you to change your announce-ment message or your security access code from a remote location, and to selectively play back only new messages that have been received since you last called in. The most advanced model includes a digital clock display and a synthesized voice that records the day and time each call was received. For added convenience, integrated models are available that combine a full-featured memory telephone with an answering system built in. Standard-size and microcassette recording tapes for use with most models are described in Chapter 3.

Speakerphones and two-line telephones

Two-way speakerphones allow you to carry on an individual or group telephone conversation from any point in the room without speaking into the handset. A sensitive built-in microphone picks up all voices in the room, and a convenient speaker volume control can be adjusted to a comfortable listening volume. The phone can also be used normally with a handset; for privacy, a mute button silences the phone when you prefer your caller not to hear you talking with someone else in the room.

A variety of AT&T two-line telephones allow access to both telephone lines. Several models are available with features ranging from built-in speakerphones to intercom systems.

9 Quick reference to AT&T wiring products

Handset and line cords

12-foot Handset Cord

Standard coiled cord connects handset to any modular telephone. Available in 13 colors.

25-foot Heavy Duty Handset Cord

Heavy-duty coiled cord is extra long for added mobility. Available in 13 colors.

25-foot Extension Cord

Extends telephone line cord for extra mobility. Plugs into any modular jack; accepts any standard line cord.

25-foot Decorator Line Cord

Extra-long line cord plugs into any modular jack to connect telephone, fax, answering machine, etc. Available in four colors.

Clear Line Cord

Transparent line cord is available in 2-, 7-, 14- and 25-foot lengths.

Telephone accessories

Shoulder Rests

Soft, non-slip surface rests handset on either shoulder. Available in standard or mini size.

Radio Interference Filter (Z100A)

Suppresses noise from AM radio signals.

Backboard, For A Wall Telephone (191C)

Covers area around wall phone for more attractive appearance.

Line Interrupt Controller

Prevents interruption of telephone calls and fax or modem transmissions. Also halts answering-system recording when any phone on the same line is used to answer a call.

Cordless telephone accessories

Replacement Battery

High-performance battery for AT&T cordless telephones with replaceable batteries.

Cordless Telephone Carrying Case

Attractive, leather-like case of durable construction fits most cordless phones; attaches to belt or clothing.

Replacement Antenna

Replaces worn or damaged removable antennas. Screws in easily; no tools required.

Cordless Flexible Antenna, With Adapter

Safer, more durable antenna bends on impact and springs back into shape. Adapter allows use with all AT&T cordless phones and most other brands.

Wall Bracket for AT&T Cordless Phones (149A)

Allows cordless telephones to be mounted on any standard wall-telephone jack. For AT&T cordless telephone models 5200, 5310 and 5320.

Telephone answering system accessories

Outgoing Message Tape

30-second, endless-loop tape for outgoing messages.

Incoming Message Tape

60-minute, leaderless tape for incoming messages.

Microcassette

60-minute tape for systems requiring microcassette tapes.

Cassette and Microcassette Head Cleaners

Removes dust and residue from tape heads to maintain superior sound quality of recorded messages. Two models available for answering systems using standard cassettes or microcassettes.

Wall Bracket for AT&T Answering Machines (316A)

Adapts AT&T answering system telephones for mounting on walls or other vertical surfaces.

Modular headsets

Three models are available for use with most popular telephones. Note: Non-electronic telephones ring with a traditional bell sound; electronic telephones have the newer, tone ringing sound. Use ATT02 for Trimline and other telephones with dials or keys in the handset.

Modular Headset for Single & Multi-line Standard Telephones (ATT01)

For all non-electronic modular telephones. Features 80-inch cord, adjustable headband and volume control.

Modular Headset for Single-line Standard or Electronic Telephones (ATT02)

For all single-line modular telephones. Features 80-inch cord, adjustable headband, volume control, mute and hold buttons for privacy, flash button for services such as call waiting.

Modular Headset for Single & Multi-line Electronic Telephones (ATT03)

For all electronic modular telephones. Features 80-inch cord, adjustable headband, volume control, mute button and hold buttons for privacy.

Amplifiers

In-Line Amplifier

Plugs into telephone line cord to allow ten-level control of handset volume.

Portable Amplifier

Pocket-size, battery-powered amplifier with carrying case for use in noisy environments.

Volume Control Handset (G-6)

Replacement handset features variable volume control to amplify sound.

Auxiliary Bell Ringer

External ringer provides traditional bell ringing sound for newer telephones with electronic ringers.

Modular jacks

Add-A-Jack Kit

Provides all parts needed to install a new telephone jack up to 50 feet from any existing modular outlet. The table model includes baseboard jack for table model telephones; the wall model includes jack for wall-mounted telephones.

Modular Jack (725A)

For surface mounting on baseboard or wall surface.

Modular Jack, Flush Mounted with Protective Cover (725E)

Mounts flat against hollow wall for attractive appearance.

Modular Jack for Wall Telephone (630B)

Mounts on wall surface to accept any modular wall telephone.

Phonemount (730A)

Allows quick installation of a wall phone near an existing modular outlet.

Outdoor Modular Jack (Z625WP4)

Weatherproof jack for exposed locations outside the home.

Wire Junction (742B)

Connects to telephone wire; up to three new wires can be branched from the junction to extend telephone service to jacks throughout the home.

Modular adapters

Dual Outlet Adapter (267A2)

Plugs into any modular jack to connect two telephones, or a telephone and an accessory.

Dual Outlet Adapter for A Wall Telephone (733A)

Similar to dual-outlet adapter, but designed for use with wall telephones.

Modular Coupler (460A)

Joins two modular line cords to create a longer cord.

Two-Line Adapter (267D)

Required to connect a two-line telephone when phone lines are in separate jacks.

Telephone Wire Plug (700A4)

Connects to telephone station wire and plugs into any modular jack to quickly extend wiring for additional jacks.

Modular converters

Modular Jack Converter (725C)

Quickly converts older, hard-wired connecting block to baseboard-mounted modular jack.

Modular Jack Converter, Flush Mounted (725F)

Quickly converts older outlets inside hollow walls to flush-mounted modular jack.

Line Cord Converter (732B)

Attaches to line cord to convert older telephones for use with newer, modular jacks.

Plug-In Converter, Portable, Four-prong to Modular (225A)

Plugs into any older, four-prong outlet for use with modular telephones and accessories.

Prewire products

Modular Jack/Prewire (725H)

Mounts quickly in junction boxes pre-installed within the wall.

Modular Jack For A Wall Telephone/Prewire (830A)

Mounts quickly in pre-installed junction boxes to connect any modular wall telephone.

Faceplate/Prewire (65B)

Conceals unused telephone junction boxes in homes pre-wired for telephones. Removable panel allows use as faceplate for flush-mounted Modular Jack Converter.

Wiring product accessories

50-foot Telephone Wire

50-foot length of durable, four-conductor wire designed for indoor use in any residential telephone system.

Telephone Line Tester With Slitter (953B)

Multi-purpose installation tool plugs into any modular jack to check telephone wiring.

Telephone Wire Clips With Adhesive Backing

Adheres to wall or clips behind baseboard to support telephone station wire.

Glossary of terms

AC power: An abbreviation for alternating current, the current in a standard electrical outlet.

American Wire Gauge (AWG): A measurement scale for non-ferrous wires (copper, bronze, etc.). All telephone wiring in your home should be 22 to 24 AWG.

Anchor screw: A type of self-reinforcing screw recommended for mounting jacks and other telephone components on a hollow wall.

Bottom plate: A construction term referring to the 2x4-inch wood beam used as a base for vertical studs in a wall.

Bridle ring: A type of fastener used to support lengths of telephone wire; usually a galvanized open loop ring with a wood-screw point.

Cable: A term sometimes used to refer to telephone wire (see "Station wire").

Conduit: A pipe or tube containing electrical or telephone wiring. Never combine both in the same conduit.

Common Connecting Point: The junction (or jack) to which all telephone wiring in the home is connected. The Common Connecting Point is, in turn, connected to a network interface.

Connecting block: A device used to connect a telephone to the wiring in your home; usually refers to a hard-wired connection that must be converted before a modular phone can be used.

Connection: Any point where two telephone wires or conductors are joined.

Dial tone: A steady signal you should hear when you lift the handset of a phone. The signal is provided by the local telephone company as an indication that the system is functioning correctly and ready for you to dial a number.

Drive ring: A type of fastener used to support lengths of telephone wire; usually an open loop with a nail-like point that can be driven with a hammer.

Drop wire: Telephone wiring that runs from a telephone pole to your home. Drop wire is installed and maintained by the local telephone company.

Electric service panel: A cabinet containing circuit breakers, switches or fuses for electrical wiring. Usually the main cutoff point for your home electricity.

Faceplate: A plastic or metal cover used to conceal the junction box or wire connectors for a wall-mounted telephone connection.

Fastener: A clip, staple, ring or other means of supporting telephone station wire.

FCC registration number: A number usually found stamped or printed on the underside of a telephone or other device that uses telephone lines.

Federal Communications Commission: A board of five commissioners, appointed by the President, that regulates all electronic communications systems originating in the United States, including telephone systems.

42A block: A type of hard-wired connecting block that must be converted before a modular telephone can be connected (see "Connecting block").

Four-prong jack: A type of outlet formerly used for extension telephones. Four-prong jacks must be converted before a modular telephone can be connected.

Gauge: (see "American Wire Gauge")

Ground: A connection between a circuit or device and the earth; the connection is used for protection and stability of any circuit or device that carries electrical current.

Handset: The part of a telephone that is held in the hand and used to talk and listen.

Handset cord: The cord, usually coiled, that connects the handset to the telephone.

Hard wired: A term used to designate any permanently wired connection; usually refers to an older type of telephone connection that cannot be unplugged.

Hook: A term referring to the switch (usually a button or vertical plunger) used to "hang up" the telephone. When the handset is resting properly on the telephone, the phone is said to be "on hook." When the handset is lifted (to make or receive a call), the phone is said to be "off hook."

Home-run: A wiring system in which each jack (or specifically designated group of jacks, usually within a room) is connected directly to a common connecting point near the network interface.

Insulation: The flexible coating used to protect wires. Be careful not to confuse wire "insulation" with wire "jacket." Insulation is the color-coded material found on conducting wires; these are gathered together (usually four or six) inside the jacket of a telephone station wire.

Insulation displacement: A term used to describe the type of wire terminals found in AT&T modular products. Insulation-displacement terminals require no wire stripping; when the wire is correctly attached its insulation is "displaced" (pierced) to form a connection.

Interface: (see Network interface)

Jack: An outlet used to connect a telephone to home wiring; usually refers to a modular outlet.

Jacket: The flexible covering of a telephone wire, used to contain and protect the four or six conductors inside.

Joists: Small timbers ranged parallel from wall to wall to support a floor or ceiling.

Junction: In this book, the term refers to a terminal used to connect telephone wires. From each junction, several wire paths can be routed to different parts of the home to connect modular jacks or more junctions.

Line cord: A type of wire used to connect a telephone to an outlet, usually a modular jack.

Loop: A telephone wiring plan in which a single telephone wire runs from jack to jack throughout the home, originating at a network interface where wiring enters the home.

Modular: A term referring to telephones and components designed for quick connection with special mini-plugs and jacks.

Network interface: A special type of modular jack used to connect home telephone wiring with the local telephone network. Usually an interface must be installed by the local telephone company.

Noise: Any audible disturbance on a telephone line.

Off-hook and On-hook: (See "Hook")

Outlet: Any of several types of arrangements used to connect a telephone to the wiring system in your home; in this book, the term is used to indicate any non-modular connection. Also used to refer to an electrical outlet.

PBX (private branch exchange): A type of telephone system frequently used in office buildings to provide service and switching among many phones.

Pair: In this book, the term refers to the two wires of a single circuit; usually the red and green wires used to provide basic phone service.

Point of demarcation: The point in your home wiring beyond which you agree to install and maintain your own wiring and connections. The telephone company owns and maintains all wiring from the central office up to that point.

Prewiring: The practice of installing telephone wiring during construction of a home. Special jacks are designed for quick installation in new homes with prewired junction boxes.

Protector: A device installed by the local telephone company to protect your home wiring from damage by lightning or other high voltage.

Pulse dialing: A type of telephone service usually associated with rotary-dial phones (although some pushbutton phones use pulse dialing). Tone-dialing phones will not work with pulse-dialing service unless they are switchable to adapt for pulse-dialing.

Ring: 1- An audible signal used to indicate an incoming call. 2- When used in the term "tip and ring," refers to the red wire of a standard station wire pair; the red wire is connected to the negative side of a battery in the central office of the local telephone company.

Ringer Equivalence Number (REN): Indicates the amount of power a telephone requires to ring; usually a number of one (1.0) or less, found stamped or printed on the underside of a telephone.

Splice: The direct connection of two wires, usually by twisting and taping, or by soldering. Splicing is not recommended for telephone wires; always use an approved terminal to connect wires.

Station wire: (Telephone Wire) Wire used for indoor home telephone connections; usually a cable containing four or six color-coded conducting wires grouped together inside a flexible jacket for protection.

Stud: 1- One of the small uprights (usually 2x4-inch timbers spaced 16 inches apart) used to support a wall. 2- On a jack designed for wall telephones, one of two small mounting posts that fit into keyhole slots in the telephone for support.

Switchhook: (See "Hook")

Tip: When used in the term "tip and ring," refers to the green wire of a standard station wire pair; the green wire is connected to the positive side of a battery in the central office of the local telephone company.

Tone dialing (also known as touch-tone): A type of telephone service usually associated with pushbutton telephones (although not all pushbutton phones use tone dialing). Tone-dialing service is faster and more versatile than pulse-dialing, and is compatible with any type of telephone.

Top plate: A construction term referring to the two 2x4-inch wooden beams used to span the tops of vertical studs in a wall.

Touch-tone: A term referring to telephone equipment designed for tone-dialing service (see "Tone dialing").

Wire: 1- Telephone wire used to connect junctions and modular jacks (see "Station wire"). 2- Color-coded conducting wires (usually four or six) contained within telephone wire.

Index

A

Accessories, ... 23, 25-28
Adapters (see also Converters)
  dual line adapter, ... 25
  dual outlet adapter, ... 24
  dual outlet adapter
    for wall telephones, ... 23
Add-a-jack kit
  for desk telephones, ... 68
  for wall telephones, ... 68
Amplifiers
  in-line amplifier, ... 26
  portable amplifier, ... 26
  volume control handset, ... 25
Answering systems, ...23
  replacement cassette
    tapes for, ... 27, 28
  types of, ... 80
Attic wiring, ... 57-60
Automatic dialers, ... 25

B

Backboard, ... 16, 23
Balcony, ... 62, 69
Basement wiring, ... 57-60
Bathroom, ... 60, 62
Batteries
  for cordless phones, ... 27
Bell ringer, auxiliary, ... 27

C

Carpeting, routing
  wire beneath, ... 56
Clip, for telephone
  wire support, ... 55-56
Color coding chart (station
  wire insulation), ... 46

Common connecting
  point, ... 39-41, 48-49
Computer modem, ... 25
Conduit, ... 43, 58
Converters (see also Adapters)
  to convert 42A block to
    modular jack, ... 31
  to convert four-prong outlet
    for modular use, ... 33
  to convert hard-wired junction
    box to modular jack, ... 32
  to replace four-prong outlet
    with modular jack, ... 33-34
  to replace hard-wired
    wall phone, ... 36
Cordless telephones
  accessories for, ... 27
  types of, ... 79

D

Desk telephones
  jacks for, ... 63-65, 68, 71-72
  types of, ... 78-80
Drilling through a wall, .. 56-57, 70
Dual line adapter, ... 25
Dual outlet
  adapter, ... 18, 23, 24-25, 50-51
Dual outlet adapter for
  wall telephones, ... 23

E

Electrical outlet, ... 2, 44, 62
Electrical panel, ... 4
Electrical wiring, ... 43, 44
Exposed wiring, ... 55-56
Extension cord, ... 18, 22
Exterior wiring, ... 60

F

Fasteners, for telephone
  wiring support, ... 42, 58
Feature telephones, ... 79
Federal Communications
  Commission (FCC), ... 2-3
Fishing wire
  through a wall, ... 59-60, 65
Flush-mounted jack, ... 34-35, 64
Flush-mounted
  jack converter, ... 32
Four-prong converter, ... 33
Four-prong jack, ... 30, 33-35

G

Garages, ... 62
Glossary, ... 87-92
Grounding, ... 44
Guest bedrooms, ... 14

H

Handset cords, ... 24
Hard-wired connections, .. 7, 29-30
Headsets, telephone, ... 27
Home wiring ideas, ... 14-15
Home-run wiring, ... 11, 39-41
How many telephones?, ... 4-5
How to use this book, ... ii, 10

I

Installation tools, ... 9, 47-48
Installing modular jacks, ... 61-72
**Installing modular telephones
  and accessories** 17-28
Interface jack (network
  interface), ... 3-4

J

Jacks, telephone
  add-a-jack kit, ... 68
  flush-mounted jack (for desk
    telephones), ... 64-65
  guidelines for installation, ... 62
  modular jack (surface mounted,
    for desk telephones), ... 63-64
  outdoor weatherproof jack, ... 69
  phonemount (quick-mount
    for wall telephones), ... 22, 66
  prewired homes, ... 71-72
  testing and
    troubleshooting, ... 73-77
  wall telephone jack, ... 66-67
Junction boxes, ... 32, 71-72
Junctions, station wire, ... 48-49

K

Kitchens, ... 61, 62, 63

L

Lighted phones, ... 2
Lightning rods, ... 43
Line cord, (see also Telephone
  wire and Handset cord) ... 14, 24
  coupler (to join two
    line cords), ... 24
  hard-wired, converter, ... 36-37
  types of, ... 24
  modular, ... 24
Line tester, ... 47-48
Local building codes, ... 58
Local telephone company, ... 2
Loop wiring, ... 11, 39, 49-51

M

Metal-sided buildings, ... 44
Mobile homes, ... 44
Modular accessories, ... 23-27
Modular jack converter, ... 31
Modular jacks (see Jacks) 63-64
Modular plug adapters, ... 24-25

N

National service center, ... 76
Noise, ... 25, 77

O

Office, ... 39, 62
Outdoor modular jack, ... 69-70

P

Paneled rooms, ... 55
Patio, ... 62, 69
Phonemount, ... 22, 66
Planning your home telephone
   system, ... 10-16
   home wiring ideas, ... 14-15
   home-run wiring, ... 11
   limiting factors, ... 10
   loop wiring, ... 11
   wiring plans, ... 11-12
Plug-in adapters, ... 33
Point of demarcation, ... 3
Polarity, ... 73-75
Porch, ... 62, 69
Prewired homes, ... 71-72
Problems and solutions, ... 76-77
Public Service Commission, ... 2
Pulse dialing, ... 5

Q

Quick Reference to AT&T
  Wiring Products, ... 81-86

R

Radio interference filter, ... 26
Regulations, ... 2
Ringer equivalence
   number (REN), ... 4-5
Ringing power, ... 4-5
Ring wire, ... 44-45
Rotary dial telephones, ... 5-6
Routing wire
   along baseboards, ... 55
   from floor to floor, ... 58
   in attics and basements, ... 57-60
   inside walls, ... 56-60
   outside, ... 60
   under carpeting, ... 56

S

Safety precautions, ... 1-2
Special-purpose modular
   accessories, ... 23-27
Splicing, ... 42
Swimming pool, ... 2

T

Tapes,
   for answering systems, ... 27-28
Telephone line tester, ... 9, 28, 47
Telephones and accessories
   (see also modular
   accessories) 78-80
   answering systems, ... 80
   basic telephones, ... 78
   cordless telephones, ... 79
   feature telephones, ... 79
   memory telephones, ... 78, 79
   speakerphones, ... 80
   telephone answering
   systems, ... 80
Telephone station wire
   color coding chart, ... 46
   concealed wiring, ... 56-60
   connecting to jack or
   wire junction, ... 52
   exterior wiring, ... 44, 60
   fishing wire inside walls, . 57-60
   installing exposed wire, ... 55-56
   installing wire in basements
   and attics, ... 57-60
   recommended spacing for
   wire fasteners, ... 42
   minimum spacing from
   electrical wiring, ... 43
   polarity, ... 73-75
   routing wire from floor
   to floor, ... 58
   routing wire through a
   pipe partition, ... 60
   routing wire through walls, 56-57
   tapping into an existing
   station wire, ... 53
   testing, ... 47-48, 73-75
   tip and ring wires, ... 44-45
   working with older types of
   telephone station wire, ... 54
Telephone wire clips, ... 55-56
Telephone wire plug, ... 49
Testing and
  troubleshooting, ... 73-77

Three-pair wire, ... 46
Tip wire, ... 44-45
Tone dialing (touch-tone), ... 5-6
Tools and materials, ... 8-9
Trailers, ... 44
Transformers, ...2, 74
Two telephone lines, ...25
Types of telephone station wire
   color coding chart,.................. 46
   D-station wire
      (two-pair wire), ... 44-45
   three-pair wire, ...46
Types of telephone
   connections, ... 6-7
Types of telephone service, ... 5-6
Types of telephone wire, ... 44-46

U

Utility rooms, ... 62

V

Volume and noise control
   accessories, ... 25-27
   auxiliary bell ringer, ... 27
   in-line amplifier, ... 26
   portable amplifier, ... 26
   radio interference filter, ... 26
   volume control handset, ... 25

W

Walls
   drilling through, ...56
   routing wire through, ... 56-57
   routing wire along, ... 55-56
Wall telephones
   accessories for, ... 23
   Add-a-Jack kit, ... 68
   backboard, ... 15, 23
   dual-outlet adapter,..................23
   flush-mounted
      jack, ... 36-38, 64-65
   hard-wired, ... 29
   phonemount jack, ... 22, 66
   to install, ... 21-22
   to remove, ... 20-21, 36-37
   types of,............................. 78-80
**What you should know before
   you start,** 1-9
Weatherproof jack, ... 69-70
Wire clips, ... 55-56
Wire junction,................ 14, 48, 51
Wire separation guidelines, ... 43
Wire, telephone (see Telephone
   wire, Line cord and Handset cord)
Wire terminals, ... 62-63
Wiring guidelines,............... 41-44
Wiring plans,................. 11, 39-41